Women of the Old Testament

A COMPANION BOOK . . .

Women of the New Testament

Women of the
Old Testament

by
ABRAHAM KUYPER, D.D., LL.D.

Translated from the Dutch
by
HENRY ZYLSTRA

Zondervan Publishing House
Grand Rapids, Michigan

WOMEN OF THE OLD TESTAMENT

Copyright 1933 by
Zondervan Publishing House

Renewal 1961 by
Zondervan Publishing House

Daybreak Books are published by Zondervan
Publishing House, 1415 Lake Drive, S.E.,
Grand Rapids, Michigan 49506

ISBN 0-310-36761-1

Printed in the United States of America

90 91 92 93 94 / EP / 43 42 41 40 39

CONTENTS

Contents

Women of the Old Testament

THE MOTHER OF US ALL

For Adam was first made, then Eve. And Adam was not deceived, but the woman being deceived was in the transgression.—I Tim. 2: 13, 14

READ — I Timothy 2: 9-15

Paul calls Jerusalem "the mother of all." In an entirely different sense the first woman ever to set foot upon this earth bore the same name, for Eve means "mother of life" or "mother of all who have life."

She is the woman who embodied potentially all that is female. In her there lay concealed as in a kernel a woman's grace and independence, her susceptibility to Satan, but her susceptibility to the faith as well. Adam represented more. He embodies not only all that is male, but also all that is human. By Eve the female also came to be through him. Out of him Eve came, and although Adam is conceivable without her because he existed without her, Eve could not exist except Adam first was and except he preceded. Of course, the world now mocks that "rib of Adam" out of which Eve was made. Yet, thanks to this seemingly absurd narrative, the most naive layman in the Church of God understands the relationship between men and women upon earth better than does the profoundest philosopher who discourses about it upon the basis of personal bias.

5

Eve was created out of Adam. He must always be thought of as the source and background out of which she arose. But this does not mean that Adam made her. Although she came from him, God created her. He did not take the woman out of Adam, but only one of the elements of human life. Out of that particle, He, not Adam, constructed woman. For this reason she too, before she appeared upon earth, existed in God's thought. God saw her, and because He saw her He created her. Eve is the product of that Divine creation.

Eve never was a child, never a daughter nor a maiden. In the instant of creation she stood before Adam in Paradise, resplendent in the full bloom of mature womanhood. Accordingly, she was not half-civilized, not one upon whom our supposedly more refined women can look back as upon the child of the primitive. She was a full and complete woman whose perfection was owing not to training and culture, but in whom it was the product of Divine creation. Woman may therefore never complain because she is not man, for she, like him, is the result of Divine activity. God's thought is expressed in her female being. It is true that Adam existed first. He was her head and the root from which she sprang. But Adam could not get along without her. He was wanting, and she was the help he needed. God created her as a helpmeet for him, but as a helpmeet who for support must lean upon him.

Satan knew that and therefore saw immediately that Adam was not to be seduced except through Eve. He recognized her amiableness and grace, but also her natural frailty. Hence he knew that she was the most temptable of the two. "Adam was not deceived, but the woman being deceived was in the transgression," says the Apostle Paul. Woman represents human grace to a peculiar degree. The beautiful in nature enthralls her more than it does man. Her sensibilities are more alert to impression of the concrete and attractive. She is instinctively not less holy or more sinful. If anything, the contrary is true. Eve's sin was essentially less profound than Adam's and, consequently, it was not her sin but his which thrust the world into perdition. But she was more susceptible to temptation because she was more peculiarly a child of nature than Adam. Besides, she was constitutionally less well adapted to offering resistance than he. Accordingly, she did not transgress alone but dragged Adam with her into sin. And, instead of loosing her from Satan, Adam permitted himself through her to be attracted to him. Eve's transgression becomes essential in "the sin with which she caused Adam to sin."

Because of it Eve's happiness was inexpressibly short-lived. At her first step she slipped. Adam did not grasp her but allowed himself to be drawn down with her. She had been marvelously beautiful. It could be said of her alone among women that she was Divinely beautiful. Now she had to leave that magnificent Paradise to enter a world of thorns and thistles. The anxiety that anticipates and the anguish that is in child-birth ravaged her being. She lost the self-reliance which God had given her. She was henceforth to be subject to mastery.

We do not know how long Eve lived but it may very probably have been for hundreds of years. Her days must have been tedious and exacting and her suffering at times terribly painful. She had been glorious once, and had lived, be it for a short time only, in the beauty of Paradise. To be thrust thereupon into a world in which nothing had yet been provided for woman must have been an awful contrast. Eve was removed from her estate. Her feminine fulness was completely ravaged.

However, into the profound soul of this woman God sowed the seeds of a glorious faith, and by means of it again permitted a heaven to arise before her. The seed of this tempted woman was once to bruise the head of the Tempter. Eve fixed her whole soul to that promise. In fact, when Cain was born to her she supposed that this child was already the promised seed and she exclaimed, "I have gotten a man from the Lord." Poor Eve! The disillusionment which followed upon that hope was bitter when, after some years, the earth imbibed the blood of Abel.

Yet, after many epochs the Angels of God acknowledged the seed of this woman in the Child of Mary. The Son of Mary was also Eve's child. It is our privilege that we can acknowledge that Babe of Bethlehem at His crib. Then, with reluctance, perhaps, but also with a glad hope we can remember Eve. Thinking of her, of that Child, and of ourselves, we can say "Mother of us all."

Suggested Questions for Study and Discussion

1. What does the name Eve mean?
2. Eve sinned first. Why then is the world cast into perdition because of Adam's sin?
3. How does the study of Eve's life strengthen our faith?

ADA AND ZILLAH

*And Lamech took unto him two wives: the name
of the one was Ada, and the name of the other
Zillah.*—GEN. 4:19

READ — GENESIS 4: 13-24

BY no means all the women whose characters are
pictured in the Bible are for that reason paragons of
piety or of modest virtue. Just as they depict man,
so the Scriptures depict woman as she is. Accordingly
they reveal three things about her: first, her nature
by virtue of creation; secondly, her retrogradation
because of sin; and, thirdly, her redemption from
womanly misery by omnipotent, Divine grace.

He deludes himself, however, who thinks that woman
is naturally more pious than man. At least, after Eve,
Sarah is the first God-fearing woman of whom we are
told in the Scriptures. And, even then, how unfavor-
ably Sarah compares with Abraham in this respect.
It is true, of course, that the Lord later gave a woman
a more prominent place in His service, and that in the
case of Mary as compared with Joseph the situation
is quite reversed. Yet, Genesis suggests plainly that
the world has not been saved by the tranquil piety
of women.

That becomes especially evident from the lives of
Ada and Zillah who, together with Naamah, are the
first of Eve's daughters to be introduced to us by
name. Ada and Zillah had agreed to be together the
wife of one and the same man. By yielding to such
an arrangement they degraded the dignity of womanhood, profaned God's ordinances, and brought new
complications of sin upon our race. Even their names,

significant as they were in those first days, tell us something about who Ada and Zillah were. Ada means "a gorgeously adorned woman" and Zillah "one whose approach can be recognized at a distance by a jingling of her jewelry." Their conduct seems to confirm the implications of their names.

When man had been tempted of the woman in Paradise, God punished her by placing her under man's dominion. God had said, "Thy desire shall be to thy husband and he shall rule over thee." Because of this curse there is expiation and new dignity for woman only upon condition that she willingly accepts the penalty. She must gladly pass through the appalling depth of this humiliation. However, faith is necessary for that, and grace, and the woman of sin refuses these. She frequently prefers to do exactly the opposite. Noticing man's desire for her, she enhances her beauty to gain supremacy over him. Such women are the Adas who adorn themselves externally, and the Zillahs who cause their golden jewels to sparkle at a distance. And Zillah gives birth to Naamah, "a stunning girl," who by the tempting lure of feminine charm induces man to humiliate himself still more before woman.

Naturally, the triumph of the woman who tries to master man is only an apparent victory. By her wantonness and vain machinations she has only fallen more deeply into sin. In reality she subjugates herself to her husband, as the polygamy which Ada and Zillah introduced abundantly proves. Since there are two wives for one man, that man plays off the one against the other, and thus the spell of her charm is broken. The evil plottings of these two women no longer result in the mastery of their husband, but in jealousy of each other. Lamech does not subject himself to them, but instead thunders a rampant song of murder into their ears. Tubal Cain, his son, is a caster of metal, and has sharpened the first sword. With that whetted sword in his hand, the bragging Lamech boasts that he will kill all who came after him, be they young men or old. Thus women foster wantonness and because of it instigate brutality and violence. Now the gorgeously adorned wives of Lamech are squatted in their husband's tent. They have meant to emancipate themselves and to refuse to be subservient to man. As a result they become more miserable than Eve. They have almost become the slaves of Lamech and they tremble when his rage is loosed.

Strange to say, the woman of sin can bear even that with patience, if only, in her wantonness, she can be desired; if only she can seem to be avoiding the curse of male supremacy. Thus she lays waste all the capacities which God has given her. By means of finery and trappings she tries to regain a beauty that has been left behind in Paradise. She employs feminine charm, which may be used to raise love to the highest possible levels, to desecrate the bond of marriage. By yielding to polygamy she murders the family, ruins her husband and herself, and injects poison into the veins of her children.

In such colors very soon after Paradise, the Scriptures have painted for us a picture of the woman in sin. No trace of womanly dignity remains in Ada and Zillah. Instead of the inner beauty which they have surrendered, they have draped about themselves an external adornment. It will remain so until God, presently, causes also the sinful woman to repent. At that time He will restore again the inner beauty of those who are holy.

Suggested Questions for Study and Discussion

1. What is the significance of the lives of Ada and Zillah relative to marriage?
2. What do their lives teach regarding personal adornment?
3. What in particular do we learn from them?

SARAH

Through faith also Sarah received strength to conceive seed.—HEBR. 11:11

READ — HEBREWS 11: 1-16

SARAH is the first woman the strength of whose faith we are asked to observe, and that specifically in her function as a married woman. Two apostles tell us this. The first is Paul who points out how by faith she became a mother (Hebr. 11:11); and the second is Peter, who pleads with all Christian women to become "daughters of that Sarah who obeyed Abraham, calling him lord" (I Peter 3:6). Who Sarah was as a daughter at home, and who as a maiden, we do not know. She is introduced to us at once as the "wife of Abraham" and as such she dies.

In a number of ways Sarah may be compared with Ada and Zillah. She, too, gives us a picture of a wife in relation to her husband. Sarah's beauty was also extraordinarily praised. And in the episode of Hagar's coming, later, to share with her the position of wife, there is suggested a remnant of that unholy state of affairs into which Lamech by his wives plunged our race. Besides, we read that she was twice wanted for a king's harem, once by Pharaoh and again by Abimelech. When we add to these facts the circumstance that jealousy later breaks out between her and Hagar, we are left with the impression that the intense misery of an Ada and a Zillah continues to fester in Sarah's tent. Accordingly, the scene is not shifted at this point from the portrayal of a shrew to that of a heroine. Sarah is also drawn to true life. In her the life of woman is presented as it was actually experienced in those days of feminine self-denial.

But one important thing distinguishes Sarah's situation from that of Ada and Zillah. Grace intervenes in the pathetic state of affairs. The mystery of faith is accomplished in her heart. And because of that faith the position of woman is so essentially ennobled that she can be held up before all Christian women as a model.

That faith does not, however, come to expression through means outside of the natural course of events. In fact, it finds in ordinary living the substance into which it can shoot roots and begin to grow. That perfect faith first induces her to conduct herself in her ordinary capacity as a wife according to the ordinances of God. That faith later fixes itself upon the Child that was to be born, and in this way upon the Messiah.

As the wife of her husband she fulfills all the demands of God's precepts. In Paradise God had said that the will of the woman should be subservient to that of her husband. Sarah seeks her satisfaction in obedience to that command. When Abraham is compelled to leave Ur of the Chaldees for Canaan, she

willingly leaves friends to go with him into the strange
country. When abducted to the harem of two strange
princes, she remains faithful to Abraham. In everything she adapts herself to his circumstances. She
receives his guests and in this way entertains angels
unawares. And, finally, she chooses to give him Hagar
in preference to seeing him die childless.

Because of this attitude she regained the position of dignity which God had appointed for woman.
Women are naturally timid, and when they come in
contact with dominance they are inclined to be afraid.
As for that Peter says to the Christian women, "Be
daughters of her, by doing well, and by being un-
afraid" (I Peter 3:6). Therefore, it is exactly by
occupying the appropriate position which God has
ordained for her, that Sarah becomes a woman with
dignity. Then, when Hagar later provokes her, she
boldly asserts her rights as a wife, and God tells
Abraham that He will sustain Sarah.

Sarah first rejected herself. It is true that she believed that the Messiah was to arise from her husband.
But she finally acquiesced in the thought that she was
not to share in that honor as a mother. Therefore she
gave Abraham her Hagar. When God appears to her
and Abraham and speaks of a child's being born from
her own womb, she still hesitates to believe it. She
persists in placing the promise upon Hagar's child.
Because of that she laughs. In spite of that unbelieving
laugh, however, she does finally grasp the courage to
join the hope of the Messiah in her own bosom.
The Apostle says that through "this faith she receives
strength to conceive seed." God, accordingly, accom-
plishes two things in her. By His Spirit He strength-

ened and caused her faith to grow. Besides, He created
new life in her closed womb.

Thus she became the mother of Isaac, and through
him the mother of the Messiah. And she is at the
same time held before all Chrisian women as their
mother. All these are urged to be daughters of Sarah
in order that they may grow in a faith as well-founded
and as poignantly progressive.

Sarah, nevertheless, had her sinful moments. Her
giving Hagar was an act of unbelief. Her laugh
represented unbelief. Because of unbelief she treated
Hagar too rudely. And the Scriptures make no attempt to camouflage the fact. Yet, in spite of whatever sins may have been done, Sarah lived by faith.
By faith she regained womanly worth. By faith, indeed, a Sarai became the princely Sarah. For, compared with Ada and Zillah, Sarah is a princess among
women.

Suggested Questions for Study and Discussion

1. In what way did Sarah show lack of faith?
2. How was Sarah signally blessed?
3. How did God recompense her faith?

HAGAR

*And also of the son of the bondwoman will I
make a nation, because he is thy seed*—GEN. 21:13

READ — GENESIS 21: 9-21

HAGAR had been stolen from Egypt as a girl. She
had probably come along from Ur of the Chaldees as
one of Sarah's considerable company. The fact is that

of Sarah's numerous maidservants and bondwomen
Hagar held a high place in the esteem of her mistress. That is evident from the circumstance that Sarah
gave her to Abraham when she herself remained childless, in order that by Hagar the Child of promise
might be born. From Sarah's point of view no higher
honor could conceivably be bestowed upon a bondwoman.

And yet this whole affair constituted a sin before
God, for Abraham and Sarah as well as for Hagar,
although least so for her. A sin it was and such it
remained for no one not married may live in sexual
intercourse with another or cause it to be fostered.
No matter how much one tries to discountenance it
by pointing to the different customs of that age, the
fact remains that the customs of an epoch can never
nullify God's laws, and all customs of the kind in
question violate God's ordinances. Therefore all three
were guilty. But in the case of Abraham and Sarah
this violation of God's precepts was coupled with the
sin of unbelief. The whole attempt to secure the Child
of promise by Hagar was the result of a want of faith
in God's omnipotence and in the certainty of His
promises. Hagar, on the contrary, was a bondwoman,
and, consequently, the least free and the least responsible.

Therefore it is not surprising to note that not a
moment's blessing accrues to this human arrangement.
Hagar is hardly become a mother before she chides
Sarah. Sarah must punish her, and she is compelled
to flee — a thing forbidden to a bondwoman. Later,
when Sarah has also become a mother, the jealousy
between the two women is transplanted to their mater-

nal hearts and penetrates even their children. Ishmael
teases Isaac. Discord arises between Abraham and
Sarah. Only after the Lord intervenes between them
does Abraham dispatch Hagar. This time she flees
because she must.

But this does not complete the episode of Hagar.
On the contrary, her appearance does not form an
episode but becomes an integral part of world history. Her influence is concretely evident today. Out
of Ishmael the Arabs sprang, and out of the Arabs
Mohammed was born. Thus all the strength of Islam
which still ferments upon three continents is in origin
bound up with the name of Hagar.

In fact, there lurks in this circumstance a mystery
which has never yet been comprehended. Very obviously that Egyptian maiden had arrived at a knowledge of the one, true God in Abraham's tent. By God's
grace faith was wrought in her heart. And because
of the promise that faith fastened itself upon the
Messiah. For months Hagar must have pondered upon
and dreamed about the thought that she bore beneath
her heart the forbear of the Messiah. For years she
looked upon Ishmael as though he were Isaac. In time,
of course, the veil fell away from her eyes and bitter
disillusionment followed.

Yet, both before and after that illusion of faith
she remained in an especial sense an object of the
Lord's care. Twice the privilege of witnessing the
appearance of the Lord was hers. The first came to
her at Beerlahai-roi after she had illegitimately fled,
and the second occurred to her in the desert of Beer-
sheba on the day that Ishmael lay dying of thirst.
It is but natural to believe that a bondwoman to whom

the Lord twice appears and to whom He gives such rich promises has a great significance in the history of His Kingdom. For the Lord does give her rich promises. At Beerlahai-roi she is plainly told that He will multiply her seed so that it will not be numbered for multitude. She is told, besides, that Ishmael's people will be a fighting people. His hand will be against every man, and every man's hand will be against him. And to Abraham God adds that He will make Ishmael prosperous because he is Abraham's seed. All this was recorded in Genesis 16: 10-12 and 21:13 long before Mohammed was born. How significantly striking it is that in the coming to the fore of the Mohammedans this entire prophecy has been literally fulfilled.

And yet this whole page of history, which begins with Hagar's faith and ends with the false faith of Islam, remains enveloped in mist. Only this can be definitely said about it, that the people which were born of Hagar have been employed by the Lord to terribly chastise His Church. But it must also be remembered that they have in large territories served to set up a protecting wall against heathendom. In Asia and Africa alike the Mohammedans have vanquished heathen strength. Not less than 180 millions of people have come to believe in one God, and in God's prophetical revelation. We must remember that the Mohammedans too recognize that Jesus was a prophet of God. Their fatal error is that they do not believe that Jesus is the Messiah and that they place a false prophet above Him. Therefore they remain stranded in the Old Testament and reject the fulfillment of the new. In its stead they place that other fulfillment which is contained in the Koran.

Is this perhaps what Paul refers to when in Galatians 4:22 he compares Sarah as a free woman with Hagar as a bondwoman, and mystically interprets them as meaning that only those who do not find the Messiah remain "children of the bondwoman," while those who believe in Christ become "children of the free." Can he probably be referring to the earthly Jerusalem which now is indeed in the power of Islam, and to the Christian Religion which no longer seeks its Jerusalem upon earth but eternally in the heavens?

However that may be, Hagar appears in the Scriptures for a more significant reason than merely to excite our sympathy for her at losing her way with her son in the desert. That more significant reason is that she appears as a link in the chain of God's unfathomable Providence. Hagar's name is entwined with the roots of the history of God's Church.

Suggested Questions for Study and Discussion

1. What was Hagar's sin? Why was it greater for Sarah and Abraham than for her?
2. What did God prophesy (and fulfill) for Hagar?
3. What is the particular message of Hagar's life for us?

KETURAH

Keturah, Abraham's concubine.—I CHRON. 1:32

READ — GENESIS 25: 1-6; I CHRONICLES 1: 32-33

AT Sarah's death the Patriarch of Mamre had become a widower. Long before Hagar had fled to the desert of Midian. After his marriage with Rebekah Isaac had also left the paternal home. Because of these changes Abraham's lonesomeness became too heavy and induced him to marry again. This time he married Keturah.

Keturah bore him six sons, namely, Zimran, Jokshan, Medan, Midian, Ishbak and Shuah. That seems strangely unusual when we remember that Abraham was approximately 140 years old at the time that Isaac married. Such a circumstance is hardly compatible with the ordinary course of events. It is not surprising therefore, to notice that those commentators to whom everything Scriptural must be usual have attempted to distort these facts. Some have disparaged the whole account as a kind of fairy-tale. Others have claimed that this marriage occurred much earlier in Abraham's life. For two reasons, however, this last explanation cannot be true. The first is that the words "And again Abraham took a wife" suggest a definite chronological order of events. And the second reason is that had Abraham had six sons earlier the events involving Hagar and the sacrifice upon Moriah would be unthinkable.

There should, therefore, be no attempt to distort the account as it is simply told in the Bible. And there we read indisputably that Abraham when he was a widower approximately 140 years old, after Isaac left him, married a comparatively young woman, and that this woman had six sons by him.

The fact that we read that Keturah was his concubine (bijwijf) in no way means to suggest that she supplemented Sarah, but only that hers were not the full privileges and rights that Sarah had. That fact

is confirmed among other things by the circumstance
that Keturah did not secure full hereditary rights for
her sons. And to the question how Abraham at such
an advanced age could beget six sons it may be answered that only recently reports came from Russia
concerning a man who, as a centenarian, generated a
son. Besides, it must be said, as our marginal commentators indicate, that the masculine virility which
in Abraham's case had been miraculously restored at
Isaac's birth, remained his until death. This is all
part and parcel of the prophecy that God would multiply his seed as the sand that is on the beach of the
sea and as the stars in multitude. Hence, this whole
matter need not detain us for a moment. The important fact remains that by a second marriage Keturah
became the wife of Abraham.

It goes without saying, of course, that the example
of a Patriarch constitutes no law of conduct, nor Keturah's marriage a rule. And yet, among the women
of the Holy Scriptures, she does attract attention as
the first woman who was willing to marry a man for
whom this constituted a second marriage. Not a word
censures the deed either in Abraham or in Keturah.
On the whole the impression is left that God's blessing
accrued to her in the rich family which she bore Abraham. Keturah appears to have been extraordinarily
blessed especially when we remember how significant
feminine barrenness was thought to be in those ways—
how significant for Sarah and Rebekah, for Rachel and
Leah, for instance. And when we remember that there
is something very appealing about the picture of the
aged Patriarch who in his declining years is sur-

rounded by a woman's love and by a whole circle of little dear ones.

Exactly because of that, too, Keturah presents a picture of a different kind of wife. She is not depicted as a young maiden who devotes herself to her husband with gushing fondness. She is not pictured as a young wife who has come to an independent position in a tent of her own. She appears as a wife who nurses and provides for the aged. Such an attitude also implies a devotion but it is a devotion which combines the love of a wife with that of a daughter. Just as the eldest daughter would support her father, so Keturah sustains and cares for the old Patriarch. But she is also his wife.

Such a relationship is hardly romantic. It hardly represents an ideal wedding. But it is a marriage, nevertheless, in which a less passionately vehement love attains very high ethical qualities. This is saying nothing about whether or not Keturah loved Abraham because of his peculiar calling, and about whether or not she shared the faith that was his.

But just because Keturah occupies such a peculiar position as a wife she has something to say to all those who have become the wife of a man by second marriage. To those who think that the bonds which unite husband and wife exist in heaven a second marriage is inconceivable. A conception such as that is, however, was prohibited by Jesus' answer to the Sadducees. From that answer we learn that the saints are not to be bound by marriage, but are to be united as brothers and sisters in Christ. In heaven the saints will live as the Angels of God. And if that is our point of view a second marriage can be appreciated, provided, of course, that it have the same high quality as Abraham's had. Such a marriage may not be a mere "living together" as the result of deliberate calculation. It may not be a "pooling of resources," to use the language of those who marry for reasons of expediency. Still less is it allowed to consummate a marriage for want of something better. There must be sincere devotion. There must be consecration of that higher quality in which love combines with a sacred urge to be a helpmeet to the desolate and forsaken.

Suggested Questions for Study and Discussion

1. What does Keturah's life teach regarding second marriage?
2. Were Keturah's children by Abraham considered to be on a level with Isaac? Why?
3. What is Christ's teaching relative to the relation of husband and wife in the life beyond?

REBEKAH

And not only this; but when Rebekah also had conceived by one . . . —Rom. 9:10

Read — Romans 9: 6-16

It was said that Sarah represented a royal figure. Compared with her it seems most natural to think of Rebekah as a typical housewife. In her younger years she was a beautiful, Oriental girl. Her beauty was unaffected. There was not a trace of wantonness in her. In fact, she represented a great deal of child-like simplicity. Observe, if you will, how she received Eliezer at the well, and how ready she was without ever hav-

ing seen Isaac to accompany his servant to Canaan in
order to become his bride. Oriental women often are
passive and introspective. Rebekah was not. Although
she came from a family of standing, she was not
afraid to soil her fingers. She herself fetched water
in the vessel, assisted in preparing a meal, and provided for Eliezer's camels. She must have been what
her name indicates, "an amiable and lovely maiden."

Her faith was not strikingly concrete. But it is
obvious enough that faith had been accomplished in
her heart. That is evident from her inclination to
leave idolatrous Haran in favor of the tents of Abraham. It is confirmed, too, by the fact that according
to Romans 9:12 she received a direct revelation from
the Lord. Again, it may be observed from her at-
tempts to secure the blessing of the Messiah for her
favorite Jacob.

Such unassuming, essentially feminine women are
often inclined to resort to all kinds of little domestic
artifices to accomplish their purposes. They are not
proud or self-assertive and perhaps because of that
they are tempted to "smooth-over" matters. This often
averts much discontent and fosters harmony. But the
devices and means employed cannot always bear too
close a scrutiny. These lead such women to resort
to cleverness and cunning and to say after they have
entirely manipulated a thing, "Hubby wouldn't notice
it anyway, and it's such fun for mother, plotting it
all so nicely."

Rebekah had this tendency. It helps us to understand why she was so fond of Jacob and why she
"simply couldn't bear" Esau at times. For, a Jew's
slyness was also characteristic of Jacob before his con-

version. Thus a hardly commendable point of sympathy was established between mother and son, but it was
one which can, nevertheless, be understood.

We are not surprised to find, therefore, that when
the matter of Isaac's patriarchal blessing comes up,
Rebekah does not approach her husband straightfor-
wardly about it. She does not remind him of God's
revelation, pointing to Esau's diverted character, and
upon that basis ask that Jacob be given the blessing.
Instead, she tries to obtain personally justified ends by
a bit of "maneuvering." Jacob participates in the artifice. He, too, has no objection to a purposeful, little
"fib." When he reaches his father he plays the role
in which his mother has drilled him with masterly
skill. Later, when Jacob is compelled to flee, Rebekah
again has ready at hand a clever artifice with which
to blindfold her husband.

The Scriptures have described all these matters very
realistically and completely. It may even be truly
argued that Rebekah's cunning was partly inspired by
her faith-born urge to obtain the blessing of the Messiah. But neither she nor Jacob are to be justified because of that. In consequence of this bit of domestic
deceit Jacob had to undergo terrible suffering. God
does not approve of dishonest means.

In spite of her unusual qualities, therefore, Rebekah serves as a warning to our busy housewives to
purge themselves of the sins of cunning and artifice.
In the sacred matter of the patriarchal blessing Rebekah felt that she had to resort to cleverness to gain
her ends. If she had not previously ruined her relations with her husband she could have approached
him openly. Ardent trust and honest eyes would have

availed much more, and these, in the case of a man
such as Jacob was, would have made the use of stealthy
avenues quite superfluous.

The detrimental results of this unsavory dishonesty
became plainly manifest in the experiences of Jacob
and Esau. Because Rebekah did not oppose, but fostered and encouraged Jacob's deceitfulness his conflict
of faith became that much more painful. As for
Esau, it cannot definitely be said that she was able
to alter the basis of his character. Yet the narrative
indicates that she left him in his ways and devoted
her maternal care to Jacob exclusively. She was punished for this by the Judiths and Bashemaths whom
Esau brought into her home and who completely lured
him into degradation. Isaac shared in that grief. What
is far more serious, however, is that Rebekah, by
the neglect of Esau's training, became partly responsible for all the misery which accrued to Israel in
ensuing epochs because of Edom, which is the same
as Esau. The wrath of Esau's enraged blood still boils
in the blood of Herod the Idumean on the day that he
mocks the Man of Sorrows.

Suggested Questions for Study and Discussion

1. In the study of Rebekah, what is the first impression given us?
2. What lessons do the relations of Rebekah toward
   her sons Esau and Jacob, teach us relative to
   the rearing of our children?
3. What was the punishment to Rebekah, and to
   Jacob, for the dishonesty which they displayed?
4. What promise of God was fulfilled in Rebekah?
   Were the means justified?

DEBORAH, THE NURSEMAID

But Deborah Rebekah's nurse, died and she was
buried beneath Bethel under an oak; and the name
of it was called Allon-bachuth.—GEN. 35:8

READ — GENESIS 35: 1-15

THE Scriptures tell us of two Deborahs. One of them, in Barak's time, ruled as a prophetess in Israel. The other served with her bosom's milk in Jacob's patriarchal family. It deserves attention that this nurse of Rebekah is also mentioned in the Holy Scriptures.

Before you lies the book of God's Holy Revelation. He gave it to His Church in order to vanquish Satan and to cause the Kingdom of His Son to come. Upon this book the future of heaven and earth depends, and, yet, in it something is told you about an ordinary nursemaid of long ago. Even her name is recorded and the place of her burial immortalized. For we read, "Deborah, Rebekah's nurse, died, and she was buried beneath Bethel under an oak whose name Jacob called Allon-bachuth, which means 'Oak of Weeping.' "

Deborah must have been a comparatively old servant. When she died Jacob had already returned with his wife and his own from Padan-aram to Canaan. He had pitched his tent at Bethel. His children had reached maturity. Jacob must have been approximately sixty or seventy years at the time, and Deborah an old woman of eighty or ninety.

Observe the tender consideration which is given this aged maidservant in Jacob's house. Isaac and Rebekah had probably graciously given her to Jacob when his family began to increase so rapidly. Accordingly, Rebekah had not dismissed her as one who had served her purpose but kept her in her tent. In Jacob's house she had very likely nursed and pampered the little Joseph and Dinah. Since then she had stayed with the family. The boys had all become matured men now. Dinah, as a full-grown daughter, had made her unfortunate visit to Shechem. And during all these years Deborah had grown in the esteem and respect of that family. Obviously, they had all become very much attached to her. She had become an indispensable treasure in that patriarchal circle. When her death-knell finally tolled, no one felt relieved "at being 'rid' of that outworn old drudge." All were touched by her passing. Great care was given to her burial. Jacob and his whole family sensed her going so intensely that tears came to the eyes of all. Jacob immortalized those tears by naming the place where she was buried Allon-bachuth, or "Oak of Weeping."

Our age likes to boast that it has reached a high stage of culture because it has done away with slavery. Observe, however, how almighty the Lord proved to be when, in countries where slavery still existed He inspired by His grace a faith which converted the bonds of slavery into those of love.

Deborah means "a bee." For a maidservant, especially for a nursemaid, that is a beautifully appropriate name. A bee is the symbol of constantly active, industrious diligence and care. By grace God converted Deborah into such a dear, quiet, faithful servant. Her example embarrasses many another maid, also some of our day who, like Deborah, are baptized and called Christians, but who, like an ant, work only for their own reward, or, what is worse, resemble the bee only in the sting with which they pierce and poison families.

By His grace God had also implanted that feeling of tender attachment to Deborah in the hearts of Jacob, Leah, Rachel, and all others. These were not only willing to be served, but they also knew how to appreciate the services. Deborah had become a member of the family. The death of a child could not have elicited sincerer mourning than did hers. She was buried as though she had been a sister of Jacob or Leah.

This, too, has a meaning for each of us. It is a shame that there are so many masters and mistresses that profess to know Christ but who look with disdain upon their servant-folk. They call it "becoming too familiar" to converse with them as a brother would converse with a sister. When their servants become ill or die they ignore it. At such times their first thought is, "We'll have to get another to take her place." The harm in a relationship such as that works reciprocally because faith is dead. Faith is dead in the maidservant who loses her devotion to her people. And faith is dead in the master or mistress who thinks that paying the salary completes the responsibility.

Suggested Questions for Study and Discussion

1. What is the meaning of the name Deborah?
2. From the record of her burial would it seem as though she had carried out this meaning in her life? Why?
3. What can we learn relative to our relation to those in our employ?

LEAH

Leah was tender-eyed; but Rachel was beautiful and well-favored.—GEN. 29:17

READ — GENESIS 29: 16-35

LEAH is one of the few women of the Scriptures of whom it is specifically reported that she was not particularly beautiful. She could not begin to compare with her sister Rachel. Rachel's face and figure were beautiful. She was a most appealing and captivating young girl. She was beautiful not according to our occidental standards, but in an eastern sense. The difference can still be observed in the young girl of our acquaintance who is of Jewish descent. In Asia and Northern Africa such feminine beauty still glows with oriental ardor and profuse, dissolving luxuriance. In contrast with Rachel's, therefore, Leah's form and features were conspicuously mean and common. Her eyes, in fact, were slightly abnormal. And Leah was intensely grieved by her unattractiveness.

It is true that it is dangerous for a young woman to be beautiful. But it cannot be denied that the girl who has no physical beauty feels quite "put out" about it. It is also true that this want can be compensated for by a rich nature, by a fervent heart, and by much tenderness and love. We know, for instance, that angelic features sometimes play about an unlovely face. But such intense spirituality is rare and whoever is not beautiful as a girl, whoever, like Leah, has something aesthetically repulsive about her, is for that reason less delightful and spontaneous. She is inclined to be constantly asking herself, "Why couldn't I have been beautiful?" The desire for per-

sonal beauty is by no means sinful. It is simply
human. For that reason Holy Scriptures occasionally
write of this or that woman that she was "fair to look
upon." By so doing the Bible confirms the capacity
of feminine beauty to bless our human life.

But it must also be said that the Scriptures offer
a sacred comfort to the Leahs. Leah, the unattractive,
was, in fact, far more richly blessed than was beautiful
Rachel. Rachel was given only two sons, Joseph and
Benjamin. Of these, Joseph was sold as a slave and
gave rise to the sinful tribe of Israel. Again, the
tribe of Benjamin was almost annihilated because of
the terrible national sin which it indulged. Leah stands
over against Rachel with her Judah, and in Judah with
David and Christ.

This is not said in praise of Leah as a woman. We
know that Laban's social, moral, and economic position
was much lower than Bethuel's had been. When Eliezer called for Rebekah she could still leave as a free
daughter. But things had rapidly deteriorated at Padan-
aram. That is most strikingly evident from the fact
that Laban really sold Leah. A man who held Jacob's
position with Laban would now receive about twenty
dollars a week. Jacob had to work seven years for
Leah. Actually, therefore, Leah was sold for approximately seven thousand dollars. Besides, Laban dealt
deceitfully, and Leah participated in that deceit very
probably because of her eagerness to win the desired
man from her beautiful sister Rachel. Evidently, then,
the moral tone of that family had degenerated quite
as rapidly as its economic status. And Leah was a
child of her environment. That is confirmed by the

fact that she later had the mandrakes sent for in order to give loose reign to her jealousy of Rachel.

However, Leah had one thing. God had been pleased to miraculously plant faith into her heart. At first that faith was still self-centered. When Reuben was born she praised God because He had looked favorably upon her. When she was given Simeon she was glad because God had comforted her in the hate of which she had been the victim. When Levi was born she rejoiced because now her husband would love her. But when Judah was brought forth she had defeated selfishness in her heart, and had replaced it by a sincere Soli Deo Gloria. "Now," she said, "I will praise the Lord."

Leah, of course, did not do that, but God accomplished it in her heart. It was not thus in Rachel's bosom. The glory of the Lord is not expressed in Joseph's name or in Benjamin's. The Lord's praise is in Judah only, for Judah means "He who praises God."

It is obvious that God's marvelous government is operative in all these matters. In his independent sovereignty He created Rachel beautiful and Leah, to put it bluntly, ugly. Out of the beautiful and ugly of those sisters a tragedy evolved. His choice is not based upon external appearances. Not beautiful Rachel but the unattractive Leah is His elect. Not Rachel but Leah is to bear Judah, and is thus to become a mother of the Christ. God's praise bursts forth from Leah, not Rachel.

This follows the rule that what repels human eyes— we had almost said—attracts God. There are two kinds of beauty. There is a beauty which God gives at birth, and which withers as a flower. And there is a beauty which God grants when by His grace men are born again. That kind of beauty never vanishes but blooms eternally.

Suggested Questions for Study and Discussion

1. Is God's blessing one of outward bodily beauty? If not, what was Leah's blessing?
2. Is it sin to wish outward beauty?
3. Can the arranged marriage of Leah and Jacob, possibly be further punishment to Jacob, for his earlier sin?
4. What is God's lesson to us as we gather it from Leah's life?

RACHEL

Rachel weeping for her children.—JER. 31:15

READ—GENESIS 35:16-20; JEREMIAH 31:15

THE last cry which Rachel uttered as she died was "Ben-oni." Ben-oni means a "child of grief." And it is in the spirit of this Ben-oni that the Scriptures depict her entire appearance.

The Lord proves sovereign and independent also in determining the extent to which each woman who becomes a mother is to share in that curse of Paradise, "In sorrow shalt thou bring forth children." Some suffering comes to all at such times, but the measure of it varies greatly in instances. There are those, of course, who, because of their exhilarating joy at receiving a child, are hardly willing to admit that they have suffered at all. But there are those who suffer terribly and excruciatingly, those who suffer almost to death. And, what is worse, there are those who die in travail. Rachel was one of these. These are they who for the life they are just giving to their child must compensate with their own. After awful anguish they sense no bliss but are thrown into the arms of death.

Who can say how intensely Rachel suffered in that hastily improvised tent when the throes of death overtook her on her way from Bethel to Bethlehem. She must have hoped that before the time came she might arrive at the city. Perhaps she hoped to give birth to Benjamin in the same place in which Mary was once to greet the child of her womb. But this was not to be. The pains seized her and of those pains the Scriptures say, "And Rachel had hard labour." The warm life-blood with which she had nourished the child in her bosom flowed away in her travail. Rachel died. But the midwife, who knew her maternal heart, called to her as she died that the child had been born alive. That was glorious music to the dying mother. Of that music in her heart Rachel voices a frail echo in the cry "Ben-oni." There was tragic sadness in that. "My child," she was really saying, "but child of woe." Then she grew faint, spoke no more, and died.

Rachel's whole soul was expressed in that Ben-oni. She was not a woman who had a highly animated, active personality. She was typically feminine, and she desired to be nothing more. To her heart being mother meant everything.

As a true child of nature she had quite captivated Jacob. He had detected nothing higher in her. But that genuinely feminine quality had appealed strongly

to him. He loved her from the start. Because of
that spontaneous love the seven years of service for
her seemed mere days to him. Even after Laban had
deceived him and given him Leah instead he could not
give up Rachel. He could not get along without her.
For her he gave fourteen years of his life. His court-
ship was a quiet perseverance which can be appreciated
only in terms of a love as romantic as that.

Exactly because of that, however, Rachel remained
less desirable in other respects. We know that she
took the images with her to Canaan. She fooled her
father. She was consumed of jealousy of Leah. When
she finally gave birth to Joseph, when she finally became a mother, her maternal pride dominated her
personality throughout.

That is the remarkable thing. Rachel's whole being
was bound up in the thought of becoming a mother.
The Lord caused her to pass away in becoming that.

In dying Rachel became a prophetess.

Jacob could not understand that Ben-oni. He saw
reflected in that name only Rachel's hard travail. But
there was included in it a prophecy of terrible suffering that was to overtake Benjamin. Benjamin was to
be completely rooted out. He was later to be led via
Edom to Babylon. He was the generation whose children in the massacre of Bethlehem were to be the first
martyrs of the Church.

After ten centuries the Lord still remembered Rachel's prophecy. Listen, if you will, to what is written in Jeremiah 31:15: "Thus saith the Lord; a voice
was heard in Ramah, lamentation, and bitter weeping:
Rachel weeping for her children." Later, in that same
Bethlehem before whose gates Rachel cried out "Ben-

oni," Herod instituted the massacre of the children. Of that the Scriptures say, "Then was fufilled that which was spoken by Jeremy the Prophet, saying, 'Rachel weeping for her children, and would not be comforted, because they are not.' "

Thus the Ben-oni of that succumbing mother's heart re-echoed throughout the entire history of God's Church in Israel. Israel could not forget the Rachel who, in dying, gave life to her child. The Holy Spirit Himself remembers that cry of death.

If in this awful tragedy it sometimes seems that pain and misery triumph always and again, then Christ's Church has found the key to that mystery in the words which she for centuries has been singing for Rachel:

> Sad-eyed Rachel, do not weep,
> Your children die as martyrs go;
> They are the first-born of the seed
> Which from your blood began to grow;
> In spite of tyranny's dread days
> They bloom in glory to God's praise.

Suggested Questions for Study and Discussion

1. What was Rachel's weakness?
2. What proof have we of her faith?
3. What prophecy was made by Rachel that was fulfilled?

JUDITH AND BASHEMATH

Which was a grief of mind unto Isaac and Rebekah.—Gen. 26:35

Read — Genesis 26: 34-35

Esau also chose two wives for himself. Jacob had his Leah and Rachel, and Esau married Judith and

Bashemath. Both were maidens of the Hittites, that
is, both came from Canaanite families and were therefore addicted to the sinful idolatries with which the
original inhabitants of Canaan provoked the Lord.
Esau's marriage therefore represents a breach of faith.
He knew very well that such marriages ran counter
to the holy calling with which his people had been sent
from Ur of the Chaldees to Canaan.

Abraham and his family had had to leave Ur because there was danger of their being led astray by
the less pernicious idolatry which had just broken out
in Mesopotamia. Therefore they had been sent to the
almost bestialized Canaan. In this beautiful country
idolatry has assumed such gruesome proportions that
there ought not to have been the least danger, that
men and women, in whose hearts any remnant of the
fear of the Lord remained, should be attracted to it.
They might unwittingly have become susceptible to
the milder form of idolatry which was practiced in
Ur of the Chaldees. But the idolatry of Canaan was
simply too shocking. Such profound self-degradation
and such desecration of all that was holy could only
inspire horror and repulsion. It was inconceivable that
it should appeal to any of Israel.

For just that reason it was profoundly sinful and
faithless in Esau to take two wives from such accursed
families. By doing so he made imminent the danger
of an idolatry as provoking as that to which Canaan
was addicted. In fact, he caused it to penetrate the
holy family.

Accordingly, Judith and Bashemath have the unfortunate notoriety of being named in the Scriptures
as examples of young girls such as the son of a God-

fearing family may not marry. Nothing, of course, is said about these two women except that they came from an idolatrous family, that Esau married them, and that this unfortunate marriage proved to be a "grief of mind unto Isaac and Rebekah." That does not mean to say that they were impossible and vexing women. There is nothing to confirm that. It is more plausible to conceive of them as having been pleasant and attractive. Esau was not the kind of man who, inasmuch as he was taking wives from the Canaanites anyhow, would devote his attention to undesirable girls. Doubtless, therefore, they were practically well qualified for life. It is reasonable to suppose that all the grief which came to Isaac and Rebekah issued from their idolatrous belief and from the sinful way of living which attached to this.

Isaac and Rebekah had been constantly perpetuating the sacred traditions of Abraham and Sarah in their home. Theirs was still that quiet, godly life to which the Lord by the inculcation of faith had accustomed the first Patriarch. Now, in their old age, these two women entered their tent. These did not share with them the fear of the Lord. They were used to the extravagant, sensuous tendencies of the heathen and they knew not God. Therefore it was but natural that conflict should arise between the time-honored godliness of Isaac and Rebekah and the shocking worldliness of Judith and Bashemath. In this conflict their son Esau opposed his father and mother. Thus the closing years of their life were passed in grief.

This narrative has been included in the Holy Scriptures for the benefit of the Church of God. The Church, too, often experiences that young men from Christian homes become ensnared in the nets of worldly women, who know neither God nor their Saviour, and who burn incense to the idols of the world. When marriages ensue upon this the sorrow that comes to such homes is palpable. After a while father and mother become old and can no longer fix the moral tone of the home. Then the spirit of the worldly, unbelieving women becomes dominant. Because of their sinful ways of living the honor of the Cross of Christ is profaned. And if children are born from such marriages only a miracle of God can perpetuate the fear of His name among their generations.

Esau with his Judith and Bashemath therefore stands as a beacon of warning to every Christian family. The pernicious evil of such marriages must be kept out of the community of God's people. Pious fathers and mothers err when they profess to be godly, but refuse to quench this fire, which because of their neglect, sometimes flares up in their home. One cannot first abandon children to all kinds of sinful associations and then attempt to admonish them. It is impossible to try to counteract evil influences when once they have been allowed to begin to function. Parents who try it are attempting to eliminate weeds which they themselves have sowed. From childhood to maturity the seed of the Church of God must be kept within the fear of the Lord and must be withdrawn from association with idolatrous influences.

Suggested Questions for Study and Discussion
1. What can we learn from this meditation relative to marriage outside of our own circles?
2. Does Esau's having two wives sanction polygamy?
3. Did Rebekah enjoy the fellowship of her daughters-in-law?

DINAH

And Dinah, the daughter of Leah, which she bare unto Jacob, went out to see the daughters of the land.—GEN. 34:1

READ — GENESIS 34: 1-31

DINAH is a girl who has a great deal to account for. Observe the avalanche of catastrophes which were unloosed because of one mistake which she made. She caused her brothers to deceitfully misuse the Circumcision and therefore the Covenant of the Lord was profaned, for at that time the Circumcision was the sign of the Covenant. Her brothers treacherously pounced upon and destroyed the inhabitants of Shechem while they suffered from the pain. Because of Dinah a whole city of Canaan was therefore destroyed, and because of her Simeon and Levi violated justice by leading away the women and children of that city as their spoils. She is also accountable for the fact that Jacob was "caused to stink among the inhabitants of the land," and was caused to flee to Bethel. And besides, she is to be blamed for the fact that Simeon and Levi received a curse instead of a blessing from the dying Jacob.

Out of just what mistake of Dinah's did all these catastrophes arise? Out of nothing more than what we are wont to call a bit of "naughtiness." She had been reared in a Christian home. But she was just a little curious about how things were being done in the world outside, and she wanted to establish some kind of contact with that world.

The tents of her father just then happened to be pitched nearby the town of Shechem. Jacob, how-

ever, avoided all contact with the little city. But this
did not prevent Dinah from occasionally glancing into
that direction. Then she often saw the girls of Shechem walking about in their gorgeous Oriental trappings outside the walls of the city. At such times
there grew in her the secret longing to form an association with those girls. Accordingly on a day when
her brothers were busy with their cattle at a distance
and she remained alone with her father in the tent, she
stealthily crept away and took a jaunt toward Shechem
"to see the daughters of the land."

Naturally, Dinah knew perfectly well to what danger
she was exposing herself. She knew, for instance, what
had happened to Rebekah and Sarah in the matter with
Abimelech and Pharaoh. And then to go alone! And
at such a young age! But, why worry! Dinah was
proud of being a little dare-devil. She was an alert
little rascal. She'd find a way out.

Sure enough! Hardly had Dinah entered the town,
begun to nose around the stores, to pick up a con-
versation here and there, before Prince Shechem, son
of King Hamor, passes along, and invites her into his
palace. That flatters Dinah's vanity and she accom-
panies him. Doubtless, after having been enticed into
the chambers of that palace she resisted vigorously
and refused to surrender her virginity at any price.
But her resistance was futile, and the end of that
episode was that Dinah was seduced.

Then, partly because she feared to return, and partly
because she was enamored of all the beauty and luxury
that surrounded her, she stayed at the palace. She
began to lend an ear to the love protestations of young
Prince Shechem.

Her desire for worldly things had enticed her to Shechem and had robbed her of her maidenhood; and, caught in the net of that desire, she decided to unobtrusively persist in serving the world.

That did not happen, of course. After slaying the Shechemites, Simeon and Levi took her out of the palace and returned her to Jacob's tent. But does that remove her guilt in the matter? "Should he deal with our sister as with an harlot?" said her brothers, and, although we detest them for their blood-thirsty revenge, we like to hear them pronounce those decisive words. But who had given occasion to it all? Who but their own sister! She had caused it, not because she was perniciously wicked, but because she had wanted to see something of the world, because she was tired of life in the paternal tent.

Unfortunately, there have been other Dinahs. Even today some could be pointed out among the daughters of the tent of the Lord. They want to see a little of the world. They want to be able to associate with them now and then, to be able to talk intelligently about what they have enjoyed. Such Dinahs do not ask for much. They ask only for the least little contact with the world, just once, for a change. No harm in that, is there?

They are just like Dinah, in other words. And even though such desires no longer result in rape and murder, yet they too often destroy religion in the home and involve the moral death of the soul. In the world's way of reckoning that means nothing, of course. But such degradation seriously indicts the Church of God, for it curses Her.

Suggested Questions for Study and Discussion

1. What are some of the results of the sin of Dinah?
2. What does this meditation teach concerning min-
   gling with the world?
3. Would you say that the actions of Simeon and
   Levi were justified?

TAMAR

*And Tamar his daughter in law bare him Pharez
and Zerah.*—I CHRON. 2: 4

READ — GENESIS 38:6-30; I CHRONICLES 2:4

TAMAR means the "slender one" and is in fact the
same name that is used in the Scriptures to designate
a palm tree. From this it may be inferred that because of her height she made an impressive appearance. But what is more important is that, just as was
Shuah, her mother-in-law, she was a Canaanite.

The fact that she was a Canaanite exposes a very
daring characteristic in Jacob's family. Although we
do not know with certainty it may very probably have
been that his other sons took wives from Padan-aram.
But of Judah, who interests us deeply as the forbear
of the Messiah, it is specifically written that he married a woman of Canaan, and that he gave Er, his
eldest son, Tamar who, doubtless, was also a Canaanite.

That Tamar was that does not necessarily mean that
she was a wicked and idolatrous person for we know
from Melchizedek's visit with Abraham that there were
some few families in Canaan who, although they had
no complete knowledge of God, nevertheless revered
the "Most High." And yet, from Tamar's pathetic

story it becomes too obvious that this remnant of faith had become seriously distorted by a severe emasculation of the moral life.

Canaan had especially succumbed to the sin of adultery which had assumed such abhorrent proportions among them that they had made it a duty in terms of their religious ritual. This becomes evident from the experience of Phinehas and the worship of Baal-peor. And we know from other incidents that the service of Ashtaroth was as blasphemously licentious. These systems of idolatry had made it compulsory that every young man and every young woman surrender their sexual honor as a sacrifice to the gods. Accordingly, their temples became cesspools of adultery. Abhorrent as it is, it serves as an object lesson which teaches the depth of the degradation to which man can fall when God abandons him to his ways.

The moral temper of Jacob's family was, of course, diametrically opposed to these gruesome practices, as may be inferred from Simeon and Levi's decisive rejoinder to Shechem's conduct: "Shall he deal with our sister as with an harlot?" And the same positive mind set is evident from Judah's answer to the news that Tamar had been playing the harlot: "Bring her forth and let her be burnt."

In this the curse of those mixed marriages becomes obvious that Judah, who condemned his daughter-in-law to be burned, was himself the cause of her guilt. Concerning her he must admit that "she hath been more righteous than I," for he was motivated in his despicable conduct by sensual lust alone. Tamar was moved by nobler motives.

It must be remembered that she had been the wife

of Judah's oldest son, Er, a man so wicked that God
slew him. Thus Tamar was left a widow and childless
until Judah gave her his second son, Onan. But this
Onan was he who became immortally infamous by
intentionally preventing Tamar from conceiving a son.
In His wrath God slew Onan also, and Tamar was
left a childless widow a second time. Then Judah
promised to give her Shelah but when the lad became
of age his father broke his promise and a third time
left Tamar in her childless state. This grieved her
intensely, for it had been her one hope to some time
become the mother of the child who was to be Judah's
son and heir. That child of her ideals had now three
times been denied her.

Had sensual passion been her only motive, she would
doubtless have enticed a man of her own age. Obviously, her purpose is to become the mother of Judah's
tribal representative. Therefore she yielded to the sin
of enticing Judah himself into adultery. Thus she became the mother of Pharez and Zerah. Therefore her
name is registered with those of that sacred genealogy.
Like Bathsheba, she becomes a forbear of Christ our
Lord.

We are slightly stunned by all this. We can quite
understand, of course, how God, for our humiliation
and instruction permits that sacred genealogy to bear
the names of two sinful women. Had it not been so
men would have said that the choicest and holiest of
the race had brought Him forth, Who was in fact,
however, the Redeemer, given by God, to sinners, out
of free grace. And yet it irks our finer feelings to see
Christ's lineage interwoven with such abhorrent degradation. It shocks our moral sense to see Judah lie

with a harlot in an outlying place; to observe Er
and Onan bestialize themselves to such an extent that
God must slay them; to witness Judah's daughter-in-
law forced to resort to illegitimate means to beget a
son. These things hurt us and we are compelled to
acknowledge that God's mercy is incomprehensible,
which permits Christ to blossom forth from a union
as illicit as that of Judah and Tamar.

But it remains indisputable that Tamar is the least
culpable of all. Judah spoke truly when he said "She
has been more righteous than I." No matter how
severely one censures and must censure the means to
which she resorted, one may not overlook the fact
that she was actuated by a sincere yearning to give
birth to Judah's heir, that she was provoked by his
breach of promise, and that she was born and reared
a Canaanite, to whom adultery was part and parcel of
the religious rite.

Therefore the thought, one which we do not completely deny, is often voiced that an unconscious desire to be an ancestress of the Christ motivated her
conduct. Neither before nor after the incident is anything disparaging said about Tamar. And the eloquent fact is that one of the sons begotten by these
means became Judah's heir, and in that way a forbear
of the Messiah.

Accordingly, against Tamar whose education had
distorted her moral sense our severest criticisms are
not directed. Judah, who proved to know very well
that a harlot was to be burned in Israel, himself indulges this gruesome sin. Judah and his sons are
chiefly guilty, therefore, and these we must severely
censure.

Suggested Questions for Study and Discussion

1. Why was Tamar's action "more righteous" than that of Judah?
2. Was the genealogy of Christ always the choice of the holiest of the race? Why not?
3. Was the course followed by Tamar justified?

ASENATH

And Pharaoh gave him (Joseph) to wife Asenath, the daughter of Potipherah priest of On.
—GEN. 41:45

READ — GENESIS 41: 45-52

PHARAOH was bent on converting Joseph into a "hundred percent" Egyptian; he intended that the young Hebrew should become assimilated into the national life. Joseph had pleased him, and Pharaoh would do anything for him. Joseph was a valuable man, in fact, to Pharaoh he was a very genius and a statesman of first rank. But Pharaoh let this be understood. There was to be no mention of a God of Israel, Who had really sent Joseph to save Egypt. Upon that Pharaoh insisted from the start; from the first he had objected to Jehovah. Therefore Joseph must prove himself to be an asset to Egypt, must become her own, must exalt her fame, he must, in short, become a pearl in Pharaoh's crown.

To that purpose he lavishes honor and treasure upon Joseph. For that reason he calls his name Zaphnath-paaneah, which means "Preserver of the Age." And therefore he gives him Asenath as wife.

From a certain point of view this marriage repre-

sents a distinction, for Asenath was the daughter of
Potipherah, Priest of On, the sacred city of the Sun-
worshipers of Egypt. And the caste of priests ranked
high in Egypt. They were sages, men who knew many
of nature's secrets, who made truly profound studies,
and who therefore contributed much toward making
the phrase "the wisdom of Egypt" a by-word in history.

Inasmuch as Joseph had proved himself to be a
wise man by his interpretation of dreams, and because
Pharaoh ascribed his unusual insight in this matter to
his identification with the mysteries of nature instead
of to Jehovah, therefore it seemed entirely appropriate
to him that Joseph ally himself with the Sages of
Egypt, and that by his marriage with Asenath become
completely assimilated with the priestly caste.

Joseph should never, of course, have acquiesced in
this marriage. The poet Bilderdijk, we know, has
sung a beautiful legend in which he makes it appear
that Assenede, as he calls her, was a girl whose acquaintance Joseph had made in Midian, and whom he
later found again in Egypt. But the Holy Scriptures
tell us nothing of this. What these do tell us unmis-
takably leaves the impression that Joseph's marriage
was a diplomatic arrangement, designated by Pharaoh
to place him inside a strictly delineated, aristocratic
society, and thus to convert him into a naturalized
Egyptian. But by becoming son-in-law to Potipherah,
the High-priest of the Sun-worshipers, Joseph became
involved in Egyptian idolatry and became a member
of a caste which borrowed all of its prestige from
that idolatry. Therefore he should have refused the
marriage.

We do not mean to say that Joseph married with

eager enthusiasm. In Potiphar's house he had proved that he could resist the tempting allurements of even as practiced a courtesan as that Egyptian woman was. Hence, it is more plausible to believe that in this instance the fragrance of the incense had made him giddy and that his young legs could not sustain the lavish luxury which had suddenly become his.

Be that as it may, the important fact is that Asenath, the Sun-priest's daughter, entered Joseph's home as his wife. And the very names of the two sons which she bore him already betray the outcroppings of the sin which invaded his tent at her entrance. Manasseh means "forgetting." "For," said Joseph, "the Lord hath made me forget all my toil and all my father's house." And Ephraim means "doubly fruitful," or, in Joseph's own words, "God hath caused me to be fruitful in the land of my affliction." Pharaoh's design to make Joseph an Egyptian among Egyptians was succeeding. Because of Asenath Joseph began to think himself as that, because of her he becomes resigned to the thought that he had died to his father's house. And this state of mind was owing to Asenath.

It came to be eventually, of course, that through God's providence that forgotten father's house returned to him in Egypt. Then Joseph himself attached the bonds that had bound him before. He felt so re-affiliated with his own, in fact, that he insisted that his bones be interred with those of his fathers in Canaan.

If only the detrimental influences of his marriage with Asenath had been buried with them. But some of her blood courses in the veins of Ephraim and Manasseh, and this blood divides them from the true Israel. Out of these children of Asenath the power in time arises out of which schism and separation are injected into Jacob's generations. Ephraim opposes Judah, and Jeroboam, Solomon's son. This issues in the conflict between Samaria and Jerusalem. It is in Samaria that the service of Baal becomes rampant; it is there that Jezebel slays the Prophets of the Lord. Thus Joseph, who had once risen to a position of might and distinction, becomes completely annihilated. The glory of Jacob's family accrues to Judah alone.

And if you ask why Joseph's tribe was so swiftly obliterated, the Scriptures point to only a single answer: "Joseph married Asenath, daughter of Potipherah, Highpriest of the Sunworshipers of On."

Suggested Questions for Study and Discussion

1. Did God's blessing rest upon the marriage of Joseph and Asenath? What proof is offered?
2. Did Joseph at heart become an Egyptian?
3. What can we learn from this marriage relative to the relations we should have with the world?
4. What is God's teaching regarding mixed marriages?

SHIPHRAH AND PUAH

And it came to pass, because the midwives feared God, that He built them houses.—EXODUS 1:21

READ — EXODUS 1: 15-22

SHIPHRAH and Puah were two stately, middle-aged women. We may infer from their names that their faces were at once vividly animated and beautiful. And we know that they were vigorous, middle-aged women from the fact that Exodus tells us that they were the heads of their profession among the Israel-

ites. Naturally, a nation which counted almost two
millions of people needed more than two midwives.
If we bear that in mind, we must conclude that Shiphrah
and Puah were the superintendents of an entire staff
of midwives. They had been appointed to that position
by the Egyptian government, for we read that Pharaoh
gave them his orders just as he might give them to
any of the officials of his cabinet.

On this occasion he gave them the awful command
that when next they assisted the Jewish women in
bearing, they should kill every child that was born a
male. That was the command that Shiphrah and Puah
were to communicate to each member of their staff.
Naturally those orders placed the midwives in a vexing
dilemma. As midwives it was their duty to do all
they could to save the lives of mothers and children
alike. Now Pharaoh's royal command compelled them
to commit murder. They were caught between two
fires. Whom were they to obey, The King of kings,
their father's God, or the king of Egypt.

The midwives did what their duty and calling demanded of them. They knew it would be sin to obey
a temporal king when his commands conflicted with
God's. Therefore they permitted the little Jewish boys
to live. Pharaoh became enraged. In this crisis
Shiphrah and Puah took refuge in a lie. They said
that the Jewish women were lively and that they were
delivered of their children before they, the midwives could come to their assistance. That lie betrays
cowardice and was most certainly a sin.

But the Lord knew the crisis that had given birth
to that lie. He did not because of it ignore the courage
of faith with which the entire staff of midwives had

chosen against Pharaoh in favor of Jehovah. Therefore the Lord blessed them ostentatiously by causing their own families to increase rapidly. He built houses for them.

Shiphrah and Puah risked their own lives for those of the Jewish infants. And yet — how reluctantly we write it! — there are Christian mothers, who, to avoid shame and distress, have deliberately killed their own children. That is a gruesome thing. It seems to say that a girl need not prize her purity highly, that she need not be particularly on guard against falling into this sin. It seems to say that, once she has fallen, she can find no refuge in her Saviour and help in God. Shiphrah and Puah are striking witnesses against such scandalous practices. They testify as strikingly, too, against those practices which no government penalizes but which are not less scandalous. We refer to those who, when they sense that they have conceived a child, apply secret, diabolical devices in order to stop its growth. They imagine that this does not represent murder but it is nothing else. How can mothers do that to their own children, when Shiphrah and Puah risked their lives for the children of strangers.

But Shiphrah and Puah have further temporal and spiritual significance for those of us who read on them.

The nursery is a very important place. A nurse or a mother can do much to guard and save the life of a baby. They can do as much to hurt and harm it. Sometimes we read that the death rate of infants, who die in their first few months, reaches the hundreds. In other cases where there is more care, more love, and more of the fear of God's name, that the death total does not reach half that amount. Some mothers and nurses have a delicate conscience in these matters. They arm themselves, besides, with reliable information. Instead of playing and experimenting with an infant as though it were a doll, they care for it as something precious which has been given to them by God. By exercising that care they have saved the life of many a young child which was threatened. That duty accomplished is so much more beautiful because the world does not notice it and God does. But God also sees when mothers do not devote themselves to their children. He observes when because of sheer vanity they dare to withhold their milk from their child. Of that we may be sure from this account of Shiphrah and Puah.

But these noble Jewish women also disseminate a spiritual influence. A nurse who fears God has a very appropriate opportunity to impart a spiritual blessing to the homes in which she works. She is alone with the young mother for whole days and nights. She finds that mother in a happy and receptive frame of mind. Such a nurse can accomplish almost anything in so sensitive a soul. The creation of the new baby is there to testify of God's omnipotence. Nor is her influence limited to the mother. The other tots in the family are quite as susceptible to her. She can exert it upon the servantfolk. And it has frequently occurred that a nursemaid has converted even a father to the seriousness of life. That is not surprising. After the nursery comes baptism. A pious nurse who is saturated with the significance of that sacrament, has a splendid opportunity to sow the seed to which God can grant the increase. Later such a nurse will, of course, leave in favor of another home. But if she served God in this way she will not be forgotten. And, what is most important, God will never forget what she did for His Name's sake.

Suggested Questions for Study and Discussion

1. Why can we say that the actions of these women were justified?
2. What should we in particular learn from these actions?
3. Does God's blessing go with the faithful nurse?

JOCHEBED

By faith Moses, when he was born, was hid three months of his parents.—HEBR. 11:23

READ — EXODUS 2: 1-10; 6:20

JOCHEBED has been included in Hebrews 11 among that "great cloud of witnesses" whose lives and activities have testified of their faith. She was a Levite by birth. From Exodus 6:20 we infer that she most likely was older than her husband Amram, for it is said there that she was a sister of Amram's father. Such a marriage would have later been strictly forbidden, but during this period of Egyptian confusion it had slovenly been permitted to occur.

At the time that Pharaoh commanded the Hebrews to throw all male-born children into the Nile, Jochebed had at least two children. One was a full-grown daughter, the same, doubtless, as she who appears later as Miriam. The other was Aaron, at this time a romping, three-year-old tot. And now Jochebed becomes heavy with child. Perhaps she had prayerfully sought to avoid this pregnancy, for, under the circumstances, maternal bliss might so easily prove to be terrible grief. Of course, it might be a little girl. But it could be a boy as well. If so, death in the Nile awaited him. It would do no good to resist the official injunction. As a rigid executive, Pharaoh maintained a close check-up in this matter. The fact was incontrovertible, if it were a boy, she would be robbed of her child.

You can picture to yourself, therefore, the conflicting storms that played havoc in Jochebed's heart during these months of pregnancy. Imagine her intense suspense, when, in bearing the child, she awaits the midwife's answer to the all-important question, "What is it?" The answer comes like a poison-darted arrow: "Yes, it is a boy." That single statement changed her maternal joy into awful grief. Pharaoh had said that he was to be thrown into the Nile.

But that very maternal grief made Jochebed a heroine. She determined to fight for the life of her child. That decision was made the moment she looked at him. Three times the Scriptures tell us that "she saw that he was a goodly child" (Exodus 2:3, Acts 7:20, and Hebrews 11:23). This does not mean that as a mother she would have been less attached to a less beautiful child. Acts 7:20 gives us a different and correct interpretation. There, especially if we compare the marginal notes, we read literally that Moses was "fair to God." Only that phrase can explain Jochebed's decisive resolve to save her child.

"Fair to God" can mean only that something heavenly, something other-worldly, something angelic beamed from the features of the little boy. To Jochebed it seemed as if he were not her own child, but that a little being sent from God lay in her lap. This conviction stirred her so intensely that she almost divined God's purpose with the child. Her faith mingled with her love, and, armed with these, she determined at whatever price it might be to rescue her baby.

We do not know exactly how she achieved this rescue during the first three months of little Moses' life. It is probable to imagine, however, that she concealed him in some secret, out-of-the-way corner of her stable or house, in some nook where he might have access to air and yet not be heard. We can imagine her going there several times daily to nurse her child at the peril of her life.

However, that could not last forever. The little fellow began to cry lustily. Then God through the intensity of her faith caused her to intuit a vision of what He had appointed for Moses. Jochebed thereupon makes an ark of bulrushes. She puts Moses into it, and appoints Miriam, her oldest daughter, to stand guard and to see what becomes of it. Miriam doubtless had food with her, too, in order occasionally to feed the child. God blessed Jochebed's courageous faith. A single day and perhaps a night she suffered from awful tension. But after that interval, thanks to God, her heart thrilled — leaped for joy. Look! Miriam is running toward the house, not alone, but with her little brother in her arms. There was gratitude, faith, and praise in Jochebed's home that day. Again she could bare her full breasts to that rescued child.

Words cannot suffice to describe the anguish which a mother suffers. It is strangling and excruciating in its intensity. A man can hardly appreciate its acuteness. It is the anguish still suffered by those mothers who say in the moments of travail, "Let me die, but save my child." They bite their lips in the pain of giving their child a single drop of milk from their inflamed and festering breasts. They watch at the cradle when burning fever and contagious disease threaten to destroy their baby. The courage is namelessly heroic of those who have wrenched their own from the clutches of villains, of flames, and of waves. And yet the anguish of a mother who fears God and loves her Saviour is severer still when not her child's life, but its soul is at stake. That struggle is still tenser. But, thanks be God's, that terrible anxiety, too, through His compassion not seldom becomes ecstatic bliss. Of such mothers it may still be said, "Her faith hath saved her child."

Suggested Questions for Study and Discussion

1. What is the outstanding trait in Jochebed's life?
2. What is the reward of her faith?
3. What can we learn from her life to strengthen our own faith?

PHARAOH'S DAUGHTER

When she saw the ark among the flags, she sent her maid to fetch it.—Exod. 2:5

READ — EXODUS 2: 5-10; ACTS 7: 20-22; HEBREWS 11: 23-28

VERY few of the Jews in Egypt lived within the palatial district. The King's assignment had sent most of them either to Goshen or to the regions of Pithom and Rameses. This accounts for the fact that only one Hebrew child had been thrown into the Nile in the neighborhood of the royal residence. Had this not been true it would be hard to read sense into this narrative of Pharaoh's daughter and Jochebed's little Moses. Otherwise she might have repeatedly found little Hebrew babies and have brought them with her into the palace. As it was she could not exactly because so very few Jewish families lived nearby. The birth of a male child to one of these was a most infrequent occurrence. Hence, it was a singular spectacle which greeted the princess on that day she went bathing among the flags of the Nile.

The remarkable thing, however, is that a very human heart was beating inside this heathen princess. Besides, she manifested a tender affection for children. Such affection is, of course, always far more pronounced in women than it is in men. It is appropriate to their nature and arises from their maternal capacities and instincts. It makes them fond of all tiny, lovely forms of life. It is the instinct which young girls and even older women express when, in the absence of a child, they lavish their affections upon the small vivid life of a bird or of some other household pet.

Hence it is no wonder that the princess was quite captivated by the lovely, dreamy little fellow whom she found among the bulrushes. It is not surprising that she could not permit the pretty child to be swallowed by the waves or by a chance crocodile of the river. In this she gives expression to nothing particularly noble in her. It merely indicates that this girl of royal birth had not lost her spontaneous feminine nature in the formal dignity of court life. She displays merely that she still has affection for a baby, perhaps just because it is such a dear defenseless little creature.

But this royal woman rises higher in our estimation when we observe what she did in addition. Had hers been a flimsier moral character she might very easily have told herself, "My father has commanded that all male children must be drowned, and although this baby is a little darling, I shall keep my hands off." She does not say that but, at the risk of jeopardizing her favor with her father, she takes him with her. To murder such a sweet little fellow would be simply too cruel.

Nor does she stop at that. She does not say "I want that lovely creature to be my plaything at the palace." Instead, she mingles affection with her love, and for months surrenders him to his mother so that she may nurse him. Thus she provided for Moses and made his mother happy. Later, when the child had grown, she does not abandon him as though all that was sweet and lovely about him had waned, but she accepts full responsibility for the lad and gives him the education of a prince.

This act of hers embarrasses many a Christian woman and more than one Christian mother. We know that these sometimes sin in that they first pamper the baby with gushing love, are at first quite "crazy about him," as the saying goes. But when their little "doll" outgrows his innocent sweetness they abandon him and neglect his training. Such conduct is not human, but appropriate to animals only. At first these, too, lavish care upon their young, but when all that is tiny, and cute, and tender passes, they push them out of their nests and abandon them to their ways.

In comparison with such conduct the Egyptian princess proved her greatness. She was a heathen woman but in her attitude toward Moses she illustrated that she was above the pagan plane. The little Moses appealed to her irresistibly as a delightful plaything. But she did not treat him as such. She planned for his welfare. And, instead of seizing him as her possession, she gave her life for her foundling.

Suggested Questions for Study and Discussion

1. What can we learn from this meditation regarding the caring for and rearing of our children?
2. Why was it necessary for Moses to have this particular education to fulfill the plans of God?
3. Could a character other than that of Moses have remained loyal to his God?

MIRIAM

For I brought thee out of the land of Egypt, and redeemed thee out of the house of servants: and I sent before thee Moses, Aaron and Miriam.
—MICAH 6:4

READ — EXODUS 15: 20, 21; NUMBERS 12; MICAH 6:4

MIRIAM is a prophetess and a singer in Israel. She is one of those women who, like Deborah, was chosen and qualified by the Lord to assist in the redemption of His people.

She was considerably older than Aaron and Moses. From her meeting with the Princess of Egypt at the Nile we learn that she was very skillful as a girl. In fact she was so apt and ready that Jochebed without misgivings entrusted her with the supervision of the little Moses. And even though she saved Moses' life, she always associated more with Aaron than with him. That was perfectly natural, of course. Moses had gone to the palace very early and from there he had at once gone to the school of the Wisemen of Egypt. Then, shortly after his first public appearance, he emigrated to Midian. Meanwhile, Miriam and Aaron were spending their days together in the quiet home of Amram. So it happened that Miriam hardly knew Moses.

Accordingly a close bond of friendship developed between Miriam and Aaron. It lasted throughout their lives and was not entirely untainted by a kind of jealousy of their younger brother. We know, for instance, that in the Wilderness of Sinai, Miriam and Aaron rose in opposition to Moses. They did so under the pretext that he had illegitimately married a woman of the Cushites. In that opposition Miriam, not Aaron, takes the initiative. That is plainly evident from the order of names in Numbers 12:1 where we read: "And Miriam and Aaron spake against Moses." Miriam was the instigator and the spokeswoman. Upon her the terrible curse of leprosy fell.

That the Ethiopian woman served merely as a pretext and excuse for rebellion becomes evident from the content of Miriam's argument against Moses. Scarcely a word is mentioned about the woman. Her whole protest is that God had appointed her a prophetess and Aaron a prophet, and that therefore they were not called upon to recognize Moses' superior authority. Her rebellious heart took offense at God's discrimination in favor of Moses against her and Aaron. True, she was a prophetess and Aaron a prophet, but the Lord said, "My servant Moses is not so. With him will I speak mouth to mouth, even apparently, and not in dark speeches." Thus Moses' older sister sought the aid of his older brother to contest his higher calling and, in a way, to rebel against God's elective sovereignty. In her, envy allied itself with unbelief. For that she was punished with leprosy. As a victim of the disease she spent seven days outside the camp. Then, upon Moses' prayer, she was healed and again received by the people. From that moment she was not, however, the Miriam she had been. Her strength is broken. The gift of prophecy has left her. Nothing more is said of her in the Scriptures except that she died and was buried in Kadesh. Nor is anything added to the effect that Israel mourned for her.

The halcyon days of Miriam's life, accordingly, are not those of the Wilderness of Sinai or of Kadesh, but they are those which she spent about the Red Sea. These were the days after Moses had come from the burning bush to acquaint the enslaved Jews with God's revelation, the days after he showed Pharaoh his signs, and finally led the depressed people through the Red Sea. During this time Miriam's jealousy of her younger brother was kept suppressed in her heart. She believed in Moses' calling. As a prophetess she joined with Moses and Aaron in their common endeavors. As an elderly woman she took her place at the head of the women of Israel and with youthful enthusiasm sang praises to God upon the dunes of the Red Sea.

They must have presented a strikingly beautiful scene in that moment. Israel stands safely upon the bank. Pharaoh, his men, and their steeds are drowned in the depths of the sea. Moses has drawn up Israel's heroes on the one side, and opposite them Miriam has done the same with the women. They stare first at the waters that have miraculously become Pharaoh's grave, and then beyond into the distance where lies the detested Egypt. Then in a magnificent chorus of instruments, psalms and hymns they burst into the praise of their Lord. Miriam was old, we said, but something of her former beauty must have returned to her eyes in that moment. Holding the tambourine and the drum in her hand, she stands at the head of that multitude of women and shouts and sings in various tones: "I will sing unto the Lord for He hath triumphed gloriously: the horse and his rider he hath thrown into the sea."

Miriam believed at that time. Pride and envy were latent in her heart. She thrilled to Moses' glory and still more to the mighty deeds of the Lord. Miriam was great in that day.

But faith, too, wavers at times. Therefore Miriam fell. Because of a lapse of faith that old pernicious hatred in her heart came to the surface again. She murmured against Moses and rebelled against the Lord her God. That God recalled her in time, healed her leprosy, and freed her from her unbelief.

Suggested Questions for Study and Discussion

1. What do we know about Miriam's early life?
2. With whom was she brought up? Did the association have effect on her later life? In what way?
3. What was the climax of her faith?

ZIPPORAH

And he gave Moses his daughter Zipporah.
—EXOD. 2:21

READ — EXODUS 2: 15-22; 18: 2-7

MOSES' first marriage was an unhappy one. His own unbelief was the cause of it. We remember how he asserted himself as a Jew and hoped by sheer might to emancipate his countrymen from the Egyptians. Obviously he had at this time not the slightest premonition of the miraculous way in which Jehovah was to use him to lead His people out of the land. As a disappointed man, Moses had to flee. Thus he comes to Midian and to Jethro. He feels disgruntled at heart. To him it seemed that the prospects of Jewish freedom were quite hopeless. He thought nothing remained for him except to die an obscure and forgotten man.

In this gloomy and faithless state of mind Moses agreed to marry Zipporah, a woman of Midian. He might have waited for a bride from his own people. But Moses was a very weak character at that time. He did not even have the courage of the Moses of the burning bush. He expresses his disillusionment in the name which he gives the son which Zipporah bore him soon after. Gershom means "I have been a stranger in a strange land." Indeed, it may be that just because of his discouragement and gloom Zipporah was able gradually to dominate him and to infringe more and more upon the sacred traditions of Israel. At least, when Moses' second son, Eliezer, is born we know that he lacked the courage against her will to insist upon the circumcision. It is also true, however, that at this time Moses had developed a stronger spiritual faith. That is evident from Eliezer's name which means "The Lord of my father was my help." But, as is often the case, the tendency to cultivate inner, spiritual values resulted in a lapse of productive, energetic activity. Accordingly Moses sinned grievously. In order to compromise an unbelieving woman he withheld from his child the sign of God's Covenant. Zipporah, apparently, was to triumph. Moses was not to conquer Midian, but Midian was to subdue Moses.

At this point, however, the Lord intervenes. On a day in which they were taking one of their frequent long treks through the country Moses and his family took their lodging in the tavern of a strange city. There God strikes Moses with a mortal disease. Zipporah sees him lying prostrate; the signs of death actually appear on his face. The conscience of both man and wife is simultaneously touched. They say to themselves that this has come about because they have profaned God's Covenant. Zipporah, who is not at home with her father in Midian but terribly alone in a strange country, sees no avenue of escape. In her despair she feels compelled to yield to her husband's wishes this one time. Because Moses is too ill to do it, she takes her Eliezer, seizes a knife, and herself circumcises the child.

Zipporah does not do that because she has repented, because her heart is broken, nor because she has been won for the Lord. That is evident from the account. She does it to save her husband's life. We read that she threw the foreskin of the child upon the ground before Moses and exclaimed, "Surely a bloody husband art thou to me." By this statement she meant:

"I had almost lost thee by death; now thou art convalescing; I have snatched thee from death's arms. For a second time you are my groom, and this time I got thee through the blood of my child." Obviously, this is the language of self-assertion and of heroic bitterness, not that of a contrite spirit. Nor are congenial relations restored because of the incident. We read that she and the two children returned to Midian, and that Moses went to Egypt alone.

It is true that Jethro later again takes her to Moses. It is also true that Moses, who had then become the Leader of Israel, neither disowned nor ignored the woman he had once thoughtlessly married. To him marriage was too sacred a union for that. After this visit, however, nothing is said of Zipporah. Neither as the wife of her husband nor as the mother of her children did she leave behind her a legacy of spiritual riches. Her appearance passes without comment in the history of the Jewish people.

Miriam had also fallen into sin. But Miriam will always retain her appeal for us as representative of faith. Zipporah has no such appeal. She is depicted in the Scriptures as an unsaved woman who opposed her husband and thus drew her family down to the lower level upon which she herself stood.

Suggested Questions for Study and Discussion

1. Why did Moses take Zipporah to wife?
2. Did this marriage leave a blessing to Moses' children?
3. Can we conclude that Zipporah is an example of faith?

R A H A B

By faith the harlot Rahab perished not with them that believed not, when she had received the spies with peace.—Hebr. 11:31

Read — Joshua 2: 1; 6: 17-25; Hebrews 11: 31; James 2:25

The Rabbis of long ago and since them many interpreters of Christianity have attempted to prove that Rahab was a different woman from her whom the Scriptures depict. They denied that she was a harlot. She married Salmon, became the mother of Boaz and is therefore included in the maternal lineage of the Christ. The Holy Apostle Paul names her as one of that great "cloud of witnesses." She is the only woman besides Sarah whom he designates as an example of faith. Besides, the Apostle James mentions her as one who was worthy because of her good works (2:25). How, then, some have incredulously wondered, could such a woman have been a harlot? How could she have been a wanton woman who yielded indiscriminately to every man who chanced to cross her threshold? Why, it was altogether too disgraceful to believe. Especially to those smug and self-satisfied burghers who with a holier-than-thou attitude looked down with disdain upon such flagrant sinners. And of course, the thought was especially repulsive to those who cultivated the habit of regarding all Scriptural characters as models of piety, to those, in other words, who based their excellence and salvation upon virtuous living.

Consequently there was much quibbling about the meaning of the Hebrew word "Zoonah" which in our

version is translated harlot. Some said the word could
refer to the landlady of an ordinary tavern. Others
guessed that Rahab had been a concubine such as
Hagar and Zilpah had been. And others conjectured
that long ago in her youth she had forgotten herself
upon an occasion, but that at this time she had long
lived in Jericho as a reputable woman. Thus they
guessed and speculated because they did not understand God's counsel for the redemption of sinners.
They distorted the story of Rahab because they wanted
to set up a scheme of salvation based upon human
goodness.

But conjecture and speculation do not alter facts.
The fact is that Rahab was a harlot. The Hebrew
word "Zoonah" and the Greek word "Porne" have at
no time meant anything else. Be it ever so shocking
to our refinement, the truth remains that not Rahab
only, but Tamar and Bathsheba as well, were all profoundly sinful, and yet they were all mothers of our
Saviour.

"All have sinned and come short of the glory of
God, being justified freely by His grace." That is the
significant truth which must be kept in mind consider-
ing this matter, a truth which applies to all alike, to
Rahab, of course but also to the most virtuous woman
we may happen to know. And unless the most piously
trained among us repents and turns to God with a
faith like Rahab's, the bestial inhabitants of Sodom
and Gomorrah will be preferred before her in the Kingdom of Heaven. The Lord Himself said that. Naturally, such standards are revolting to humanistic con-
ceptions of virtue. But they are the only standards of
the Holy Scriptures all the same. In fact, the matter

can be still more poignantly stated. Rahab was not
a harlot first and a woman of faith after that. She
was both at the same time. Faith was hers and func-
tioned in her at the same time in which she received
strange men into her home. Not until God caused the
walls of Jericho to fall and with them Rahab's house
of prostitution did she become converted from her sin.
After that she married a Prince of Israel. But it is
because of the faith which operated in her at the same
time in which she indulged her venal wantonness, that
she is named and immortalized by the Apostle as a
heroine of faith.

The people who in Rahab's time most frequently
used such houses of prostitution were the traveling
merchants. From these she had repeatedly heard of
the marvelous nation which was approaching from
Egypt, and of the God of Israel who had perfected
such striking miracles. God employed these merchants
to preach His word. Israel was at this time inces-
santly murmuring. It had become necessary for God
to smite Miriam with leprosy. Because of his sin with
Zipporah Moses himself had become afflicted with mortal illness. And while these things were going on
among His Chosen People it pleased God to accept this
harlot in grace. Doubtless, there were hundreds of
virtuous women in Jericho. These were all passed by.
God's mercy had compassion upon this sinful strumpet
alone.

It is possible that this more pious attitude had
been developing in Rahab's heart for years. Perhaps
she was diverted from the idolatries of Jericho by the
fact that she had heard of that other God, a God not
carved from stone, but one who performed marvelous

miracles and proved capable of redeeming his people. At this juncture in the growth of her faith two representatives from that God visit her. They come to her house not to indulge sin with her, but to prepare the way for God's people. Now Rahab's faith becomes decisive and positive. She feels that she cannot resist that God and she has no desire to do so. She regards her visitors as His official ambassadors. She risks her life for theirs. Perhaps the Prince of Jericho will behead her for it in the morning. He could not be expected to be lenient with a harlot. Down with those fears. These men must be saved. And Rahab saves them, not because of expediency, nor because of human pity, but because they have been sent from the Most High God.

Rahab did what she did for God's sake. The first fruits of her faith become evident at once. Her previously frozen heart melts, for she again thinks of her father and mother and asks whether these, too, may be saved.

Israel's army stations itself around Jericho. But in the whole city none but the harlot recognizes the approach of God in that army. She opens the window and throws out the crimson cord. She believes, and her redemption is sure. God incorporates her into the holy lineage of His only-begotten Son. In doing that He does not approvingly ignore her adultery. Never for a moment think that. St. Paul would say, "God forbid!" He does so in order to teach us that His grace is omnipotent, and that it is able and willing to redeem even the most profoundly sinful. And He tells us, besides, that because He has stopped the conflagration of sin in us from spreading out, we may not

in smug self-righteousness look down with haughty
disdain upon the sins of others.

Suggested Questions for Study and Discussion

1. Why are the lives of so many women outside of
   Israel recorded in the Word of God?
2. Could these women, even in Old Testament times,
   be saved?
3. How do you account for the fact that Rahab had
   knowledge of the true God?
4. What was the reward of her faith? Do "good
   works" receive their reward?

DEBORAH

*Until that I Deborah arose, that I arose a mother
in Israel.*—JUDGES 5:7

READ—JUDGES 4:4, 5:5

Deborah is the Jeanne d'Arc of Israel's astonishing
history. Israel's history is astonishing. Hardly ever
did a nation fall into idolatry as frequently, as rapidly,
and as profoundly as they. At such times they seemed
to lose all sense of national consciousness and to completely surrender their prestige and honor. But there
is a compensating aspect in this matter which is equally
striking. No nation ever possessed such an indefatig-
able national resilience as was theirs. By means of
it they as frequently, as rapidly, and as conclusively
revived again from their spiritual and political disintegration. That was owing to the fact that this resilience was not a humanly cultivated quality but a gift
of God. That God's predestination was each time the
cause of Israel's restoration becomes perfectly evident
from this story of Deborah and her days.

Almost all the plains of Palestine had again succumbed to the strength of the Canaanites. Jabin, their king, resided at Hazor, and ruled over Israel by virtue of an armed force. His army was strong, well-equipped, and especially dreaded because of its nine hundred chariots of iron. Against these the efforts of any infantry proved futile. Consequently the country-folk who dwelt in these plains had to pay tribute to Jabin. They lived in a condition of slavery, and that under circumstances even more severe than those to which the Turks long forced the Christians to submit. Only the people in the hill-country had been able to preserve a kind of freedom, simply because Jabin's chariots of war proved useless here. In fact, those who lived upon the highlands of Ephraim still possessed a degree of organization. It was owing to the heroic courage which had been inspired in the hearts of the people.

The wife of Lapidoth had displayed the ability to inspire that courage. She lived under the palm tree between Ramah and Bethel. Her name was Deborah, and she was reckoned a "mother in Israel." Her qualities were many and various. She not only possessed mental acumen and common sense but was also a woman to whom the Lord had given the gift of prophecy and song. Because of these abilities she had succeeded in calling the hill-folk back to Jehovah. She reminded them of their significant history in Egypt and Sinai and prophesied the coming of better days. As a judge she had determined justice and given frequent advice. Thus her reputation had become generally known. Israel again found a common center in this remarkable woman. Her songs passed from mouth

to mouth and resounded from every hill. Thus she
inspired heroic confidence and awakened the glad hope
of freedom in every tribe. With Barak's aid she even
built up a small standing army among the people. By
means of guerrilla-warfare she trained Barak in gen-
eralship and her army in military preparedness. Obviously, she was active and qualified for things ideal
and practical alike.

For that reason Deborah was greater than Kenau
Hasselaar, and greater even than Jeanne d'Arc. Deborah was called by God. She proved to be unusually
wise and tactful. She had not leaped into full glory
at once, but had by many years of exertion and organ-
izing activity prepared Israel for her war of independence. After these had been completed, she acted quickly
and decisively.

She saw that the strategic moment had come. She
called Barak and told him that the time was ripe for
action. He was to enlist ten thousand men from Naph-
tali and Zebulon and to station them upon the mountain ridge of Tabor, which meandered from Ephraim
down to the river Kison. She promised that when he
had done that she herself would come to the camp.
In the meantime she directed the other hill-folk of
the region to take possession of the remaining mountain passes. She knew Jabin's haughty boldness and
she knew that the Lord would induce him to enter
the dangerous valley of the Kison in spite of the rainy
season.

Everything happened as she had directed. Barak
gathered his ten thousand men upon Tabor. The others
blocked the passes of the North-country. Deborah
came to the camp. When Jabin heard of these efforts

toward freedom, he immediately took his men and his chariots and made for the valley of the Kison. There followed upon the slopes of Tabor a piece of heroism which seeks its equal in all history. Completely defying death, this poorly equipped infantry threw itself with such relentless force upon the mighty hosts of Jabin, that these shrank back and were thrown against the turbulent Kison. God sent thunder and lightning, and a cloudburst which swelled the river so that it broke from its banks and completely disorganized Jabin's army. Israelites pounced upon them from every mountain pass and completely annihilated their enemy.

God accomplished that through one woman. Barak did not achieve it, for, if he had, his praises would have been sung by all the people. But God achieved it through a woman so that because of her weakness His Omnipotence might more gloriously be made manifest.

Deborah was mighty because the Spirit of the Lord, moved, qualified and inspired her. God kindled a fire in her heart. Sparks from it flew to all parts of Israel's hill-country. Heroic courage flared up in every heart. Sometimes, in some quiet, secluded village, the Lord still selects a woman and implants in her the fear of His name. He appoints her to be a "Mother in Israel." Inspiring influences radiate from her and awaken the sleeping ones until such time as God shall cause the Light of His Christ to illumine them.

Suggested Questions for Study and Discussion

1. Do you suppose, since we read of no sins, that Deborah was sinless?

2. What characteristic do you admire most in Deborah?
3. Would God's use of Deborah as a Judge in Israel imply that women could preach today?

JAEL

Blessed above women shall Jael the wife of Heber the Kenite be, blessed shall she be above women in the tent.—JUDGES 5:24

READ—JUDGES 4:17-24; 5:24-31

Jael reminds us of Judith of Bethulia, who drove a sword through Olofernes' throat as he slept.

She was the wife of Heber the Kenite. The Kenites were not true Israelites, but were the descendants of Moses' wife. Because they were a roaming nomadic people they lived in tents. In Deborah's days they had camped at the foot of Mount Tabor. In fact, they were situated very near the place where Barak and Deborah had destroyed Jabin's mighty army, including his nine hundred chariots of iron. Jabin had permitted the Kenites to stay in the country because he hoped they would prove to be his ally against the Israelites whom he hated fiercely. But they disappointed Jabin's hopes. From the first, perhaps because they remembered Moses' great deeds, the Kenites had sided with Israel.

Jael, too, was Israel's ally. She rejoiced when she heard of Barak's victory and would have wept had she heard that Sisera had defeated Israel with his chariots. Jael received the honor that Barak would like to have had. By her hand, as though by a judgment of God, Sisera, Israel's cruel oppressor, was killed. Barak would have had that honor just as David had that of slaying Goliath if he had not dallied and hesitated on the day Deborah had asked him to attack Jabin. But because he had hesitated at that time, Deborah, as a prophetess, told him the word of the Lord: "The journey that thou takest shall not be for thine honour, for the Lord shall sell Sisera into the hand of a woman" (Judges 4:9).

Therefore we may not disapprove of Jael's act in killing Sisera. We remember that an Israelite once took a harlot of the Midianites into his tent. On that occasion Phinehas pinned them together by a thrust of his javelin. For that he was praised because his zeal for Jehovah had induced him to do it. Jael's act is not more censurable than his, for she was accomplishing the Lord's judgment upon Sisera. Hence it is written in Deborah's song: "Blessed above women shall Jael the wife of Heber the Kenite be, blessed shall she be above women in the tent."

Our marginal commentators and all early interpreters are therefore correct in saying that Jael killed Sisera not because of a personal impulse, but because the Spirit of the Lord had kindled in her a holy zeal for Jehovah. But from this may not be inferred that the means she employed to realize her fervor were also approved by God. In this connection the acts of Phinehas and David are no longer analagous. These did not resort to ethically disgraceful means to accomplish their purposes. Phinehas made his attack openly, and David ventured to approach the giant Goliath with a sling. These men relied upon God to help them.

Jael did not have this reliance upon God. It is true that she felt an irresistible impulse to kill the professed enemy of God and his people. But she lacked faith in the fact that God would help her, and hence she lacked the courage to attack Sisera fairly and openly. She did not, as David did, defiantly hurl at him the charge that he had blasphemed the living God. Accordingly, the fame of David and Phinehas lived on, but Jael's faded away.

Obviously, Jael was not a coarse and a crude woman. She was most unlike the dames de Halle who fiercely displayed the tiger in their nature during the French Revolution. She simply lacked courage; she did not dare attack Sisera fairly· Jael adopted the proverb "Whoever is not strong, must be clever." She resorted to artifice. She met him at the door with a face all beaming welcome. She gave him a drink and spread out a bed for him to rest on. Sisera completely surrendered to her spontaneous hospitality and fell asleep without misgivings. Then she covered him with a mantle, took a pin from the tent, and drove it through his temples.

Thus the judgment of the Lord was accomplished upon Sisera. The zeal of the Spirit urged her to do it, but she did it by foul and reprehensible means. She remains forever censurable for that. Jael killed Sisera as an assassin would kill his victim, but not as a champion of the Lord out to destroy the arch-enemies of God. To be zealous for God is good and is commanded by the love of His name. But, whoever would do things for the Lord must let God designate the means. Jael is to be blamed because she did not do that.

Suggested Questions for Study and Discussion

1. How was Jael related to the people of Israel?
2. Was Jael's deed a noble one?

3. If you had been Jael, how would you have gone
   about the killing of this King?
4. Did God's blessing rest upon Jael for this act?

JEPHTHAH'S DAUGHTER

READ — JUDGES 11:29-40; HEBREWS 11:32

Perhaps it no longer needs be argued that Jephthah did not actually burn his daughter. Human sacrifice was a gruesome thing in Israel. Jehovah was not
a Moloch to whom fathers sacrificed their children
upon an altar. Besides, everything in the narrative
argues against such an interpretation. Would a child
who was to die, ask for two months of postponement
and then spend these two months apart from her parents? And, had death really awaited her, why should
she have cared to bewail her virginity? And, what
under such circumstances could conceivably be the
sense of that other added statement "And she knew
no man?" Or again, why would the daughters of
Israel have cared to lament for her four days of each
year?

Consequently (just as our marginal commentators
have always maintained in opposition to Luther), there
is no doubt about it that Jephthah's sacrifice consisted
of this that he was never to allow her to marry but
was instead to dedicate her to the service of the Tabernacle. Not by choice but because of her father's vow,
Jephthah's daughter was to live at that Tabernacle
as one dedicated to the Lord. She was to live there,
segregated from her friends and family, until her
death.

We have no right to superimpose the Pagan tale of Iphigenie upon this Biblical narrative.

Jephthah had defeated Ammon and had reached the acme of a glorious career. By his rash vow he in that same moment robbed himself of his daughter and forever deprived her of the joy of life. That is the role which Jephthah's daughter assumes as she appears before us. She appears as the victim of her father's vow. The truly tragical appeal of her character arises from the fact that without any attempt at a prudish concealment of her sadness, she willingly acquiesces in her destiny.

Jephthah's daughter was by no means a lass who might be expected to voluntarily seek out the cell of the cloister. That is perfectly obvious from the way in which she goes to meet her father. A reticent, introspective girl would have stayed at home, would perhaps have secreted herself behind the door, and then have rushed to embrace him as he entered. But not she. She was full of energy and vivacity, of intense fervor and enthusiasm. She called all the maidens of Mizpeh together and told them to be sure to bring their cymbals and drums. Together with these she ran to meet the conqueror even before he had entered the city. And she did so, singing, dancing, and rejoicing all the way. She must, therefore, have been a girl who was "just full of life." Her eager, sparkling eyes captivated as they look squarely into the world's face. Besides, there was an eager urge in her soul to enter that world, to praise Jehovah's strength there, and to sing of the glory of her father whom He had chosen.

The narrative suggests that she had just reached

the age at which such daughters usually married. We
may think of her, consequently, as no longer a girl
and yet not quite a woman. In short she was a picture of genuine, feminine fullness in all its beauty and
all its hope.

But there is more to be said. She had suddenly
become the daughter of Israel's hero, of him who had
emancipated Israel from Ammon. Doubtless, therefore, many a young man of high social standing kept
his eye fixed upon her. It is most likely that those
eager, joyous young soldiers who returned from defeating Ammon fell helplessly before her feet in sheer
wonderment. How could they have done anything else
at witnessing her colorful approach? For she came
strumming, and singing, and dancing at the head of
Mizpeh's choicest daughters.

Her father's words struck her with the sudden-
ness of thunder and with the effect of a thud. "Alas,
my daughter, I have made a vow unto the Lord and
according to that vow I must segregate you from the
world unto death." Jephthah himself sensed the awful
tragedy of it. He saw his vivid, ardent daughter and
he knew he had to extinguish that spontaneous glad-
ness and convert it into sadness. He knew that he
had cut off the glorious future that was just opening
up before her.

How did she react to it? By playing an artificial
role and falsely asserting "That is quite all right, father, I am sure I shall enjoy the life of seclusion?"
By no means. That moment found her as real and
genuine as ever. She did not mope about it but neither
did she conceal that she sensed the sacrifice of it.
She said "If thou hast opened thy mouth unto the

Lord, do to me according to that which hath proceeded out of thy mouth." But she added in the same breath "Let me alone two months, that I may go up and down upon the mountains, and bewail my virginity."

She was given those two months. She took her best friends with her to the neighboring hills, perhaps to a summer cottage which Jephthah possessed there. There she tried to find herself, and to adjust herself to the startling change which faced her.

She had wanted to marry and to enjoy a full, rich life. That was denied her. She was to live in seclusion, isolated from her family and her friends. She was condemned to run the course of her years tediously, forsaken and alone. That might have constituted an ideal to some sentimentally fanatic girl, but to this vividly vital and happy lass it was by no means that. It represented the greatest sacrifice she could possibly bring. She brought it willingly. Her father had made a vow and it could not be broken. Hence, she did not complain although she wept bitterly. Then she went into her life-long seclusion with contentment.

Suggested Questions for Study and Discussion

1. Do you think that Jephthah fulfilled his vow to God?
2. Do you think, after God has wrought so much for us, that we should make such vows? Are they just to ourselves and others?
3. What does God wish us to learn from this recorded event?

MANOAH'S WIFE

And there was a man of Zorah, of the family of the Danites, whose name was Manoah; and his wife was barren and bare not.—JUDGES 13:2

READ —JUDGES 13

The wife of Manoah is another woman of the period of the judges who attracts our attention. Like Sarah and Hannah she lived for a time in a state of barrenness. She is therefore one of a trio in Israel's early history who first felt the intense sorrow and disappointment of a childless state, and who then, after an especial announcement from the Lord, bathe in the luxuriance of maternal joy. Isaac, Samson and Samuel are the three men who owe their birth to the severe conflict of faith which these mothers were compelled to fight.

Samson's mother was married to Manoah, a man of the tribe of Dan. She lived with him at Zorah. This couple evidently lacked none of the necessities of life, for their stables housed their own cattle. They seem to have been well-to-do people. But the true joy of having a child of their own had up to this time been denied them.

However, on a certain day the wife had gone into the fields alone and at this time an apparition appeared to her. It was an Angel of the Lord, one very similar to the three who had appeared to Abraham in the plains of Mamre. Manoah's wife regarded him as a man, although she later reported that his face shone "very terribly." And although she had never seen him before, she learned that this stranger knew her most intimate conflicts, for, without further introduction he mentioned the subject of her barrenness. Then he gave her the unexpected assurance that she was to have a child not long after. He told her, besides, that her child was in a special sense to be a servant of the Lord, that he was, in fact, to be a Nazarene of God. Because of that he advised her to abstain from the fruit of the vine during the period of her pregnancy.

Naturally, Manoah's wife, upon arriving home, had to tell her husband all about this strange meeting. She said she had not dared to ask who he was, and that he had not imparted to her his name. Of course, her husband was quite astonished, and just as she had thought he surmised that the man had been an Angel of the Lord. Who but an angel could make such promises? And yet, this reasoning did not entirely satisfy Manoah. In obedience to a pious impulse he fell upon his knees and asked that God permit that same Angel to appear to them once more.

That prayer was answered. Again Manoah's wife went alone into the fields and again that resplendent form appeared to her. This time she, too, became excited, and she ran home to call her husband. He came quickly, and now both stood before the Angel. He seemed to be that and yet such splendor beamed from his human form that they hardly knew how to interpret it. However, the suspense became unbearable for Manoah and he asked boldly, "Art thou the man that spakest to the woman?" Upon being answered affirmatively, Manoah became hospitable and offered to prepare a kid for him. But the angel refused saying "Though thou detain me I will not eat thy bread, and if thou wilt offer a burnt offering

thou must offer it unto the Lord." Manoah knew then
that he was an Angel, but he did not know that He
was the Messiah himself. And yet, in answer to the
question "Who art thou?" he is told that His name
was Wonderful. Manoah prepared a sacrifice, and as
the flames rose toward heaven, the Angel soared with
them. Then they fell upon their knees before the
Lord because they saw and recognized that he was
truly an Angel of the Lord.

The vision passed but not the words which the
Messiah had spoken. Not long after the woman became pregnant and when her days were fulfilled she
gave her people Samson. He was the deliverer promised by God, who was to wreak vengeance upon the
Philistines. God directed these matters as He did not
because of Manoah and his wife but because of Samson.

The Lord had heard the cries of His people. All
the tribes were murmuring and complaining. Despair
had seized the hearts of many because the deliverer
did not come. And ever while these complaints were
soaring, the Lord had already provided the redemption. Samson had been born. Samson's mother remained barren for years in order that God's Providence should be more plainly evident. She did not
give Israel her redeemer, but the Lord gave him. And
in this story God shows us besides how the future of
that child was prepared by the spiritual and physical
conflicts of his mother. Samson was to be a hero of
faith, and therefore she first had to fight the conflict
of faith. He was to be a Nazarene of God and therefore she was to abstain from wine during the period
of her pregnancy. Just that intimately, even before

birth, the body and soul of a mother can lastingly
affect those of her child.

Suggested Questions for Study and Discussion

1. Why did God so often choose to supply His
   people with prophets and deliverers from women
   who had long been barren?
2. Do you suppose that Manoah's wife was a be-
   liever?
3. What does the term "nazarene" mean?

DELILAH

*And it came to pass afterward, that he loved a
woman in the valley of Sorek, whose name was
Delilah.*—JUDGES 16:4

READ—JUDGES 16:4-20

DELILAH, who had built her house upon the banks
of the Sorek, is a woman who creates the greatest
aversion in the minds of all who read of her.

Samson is the hero of God. His appearance as a
redeemer in Israel rema ns a mystery. He was chosen
and equipped by God to accomplish His purposes in
strikingly unusual ways. But Samson, the dauntless
hero, had one basic sin. He could not resist a woman's
charm. We read that first one woman and then another took advantage of this deep-seated weakness in
him to lure him into submission to her. Of these
women Delilah was the most effective.

Even in Gaza Samson had almost become the victim of his sensuous nature. There, too, he had visited
a harlot and had become the prey of the Philistines.
But the Lord still had compassion on him and enabled

him to lift the gate of the city, bar and all, out of its socket. Thus he escaped even before the Philistines had awakened. But Samson's prodigious masculine energy so completely mastered him that he could not purge himself of this weakness. Hardly had he escaped from Gaza before he again entered the house of a harlot. This time he stopped at the home of Delilah, at Eshtaol, in the valley of Sorek.

Delilah had a sweet-sounding name, one such as vain women like to assume even though they have been given another. And in her home Samson found what proved to be worse than his death. Like all practiced courtesans, she was mistress of the art of feigning love in spite of being quite untouched at heart. By a display of fondness and intimacy she brought Samson to his doom. She had but one purpose and that was to get money. The Philistines promised her an abundance of that upon the condition that she betray Samson into their hands. When she knew that, she knew as well that she would spare no treachery to catch him in her snares.

The deceitful play of treacherously feigned love began. She loved Samson dearly, she said. But, of course, that was not enough. He must love her too, and must love her with his whole heart. Wanting that, she craftily argued, how could a sincere, reciprocal love-relationship ever develop?

By protestations such as these she captivated Samson's heart. To him it seemed that his sin became less sinful in that he had given himself to a woman, who, in spite of her illicit practices, had an ideally beautiful conception of love. She urged him to become confidential in this way. Observe how she went about

it. Samson ought not to keep any secrets from his
dear Delilah, she said. Then she added, "How canst
thou say 'I love thee,' when thine heart is not with
me?" The despicable serpent that she was! One
marvels that even she could dare say such a thing.

She progressed. Samson was weakening to her
charms. At first she had not entirely trusted her and
had fooled her several times. But he never freed himself from the intoxication which her wiles induced.
Each successive temptation only incited him to display
his supernatural strength in another and more striking way. The source of that strength, he knew, was
his hair. But first he permitted himself to be bound
with green twigs and with new ropes. These he broke
as though they had been charred rags. The third
time he already mentioned his hair and allowed it to
be woven into the web on the loom. But the Lord
remained with him and again he escaped.

At this juncture Delilah extended her choicest bait.
She pretended that she had been neglected and trifled
with by an unrequitting love. Samson succumbed to
that. He pointed to his locks and betrayed the honor
of a Nazarene to that infamous woman. Then the
Lord departed from him and he became the Philistines'.

Base Delilah gloated over that. It represented the
triumph of her indifferent love-making and her un-
scrupulous tongue. She had done what a battalion of
Philistines could not have achieved. She gloried in
that and boasted of it. Her malicious soul reveled in
the thought that she could give a defenseless Samson
into the Philistines' hands. She watched as they bound
him and led him out of the house. Then she turned

to the large sums of money which she had been given as the reward for her treachery.

In all these matters we do not mean to justify Samson. As a hero of the Lord he had no right to be visiting harlots at Gaza and at Sorek. He sinned profoundly in yielding to these insidious women. He had forgotten to fear God.

In spite of that, however, Delilah stands out as an infamous woman from the pages of the Scriptures. She was that because of her sinful ways of living, naturally, but even more so because she trifled with love for the sake of lucre. She coyly flattered Samson and acted as though she thought love was too noble and sacred a thing to receive a half-hearted consideration. And all the while she kept a police force quartered in her rooms and awaited the moment in which she could surrender her lover into his enemies' hands.

It is true that Delilah misused her feminine appeal to an unusually disgraceful extent. Yet, every woman is essentially like Delilah who feigns love and indulges vanity and coquetry in order to attain selfish ends. Feminine charm and the appeal of love are also gifts of God. Woman has received them from her Creator. Because of that God will certainly punish those, who, by deliberately trifling, misuse these fairest and most effective of gifts.

Suggested Questions for Study and Discussion

1. Was Samson justified in visiting these strange women?
2. What was the great sin of the life of Delilah?
3. Is it Biblical to sell love for money, as Delilah did with Samson?

NAOMI

And she said unto them, Call me not Naomi, call
me Mara: for the Almighty hath dealt very bitterly
with me.—RUTH 1:20

READ — RUTH 1

NAOMI means the "pleasant one." Now that you
have tired of observing and perhaps been hurt by the
Tamars and Rahabs and Delilahs, Naomi will, indeed,
strike you as a friendly and amiable woman. Not all
the persons who have been included in the sacred genealogy of the Christ have been Naomis and Ruths. For
our humiliation and appropriate self-condemnation the
Lord compels us to acknowledge that, because of our
sin, the Tamars and Rahabs and Bathshebas have their
place in that lineage. Hence, it re-enlivens our souls
and refreshes us when God permits us momentarily
to observe nobler characters than they. Greater beauty
is reflected by the eyes of some of these, than ever the
sun conjured up in those of an Oriental girl.

Naomi has such innate nobility of character that
she immediately elicits from us our most sincere sympathy. That is partly owing to the fact, as it seems,
that her character was purged by suffering.

As the young wife of her husband Elimelech, she
had been compelled because of the famine to flee from
Bethlehem and to seek her sustenance in a foreign
country. Even this constituted a real sacrifice to Naomi. She loved the people of God and felt strongly
attached to the marvelous tradition of her race. In
fact, the ideals of Israel tugged so relentlessly at her
heart that she returned to Bethlehem later as a widow.
But she returned as a widow, for one catastrophe after

another overtook her. After the famine at Bethlehem and the exile to Moab she was compelled to experience the death of her husband. That left her desolate and lonesome with her two sons. But even that was by no means the extent of her suffering. Because of these two children she was to drink the cup of grief to the dregs. Both Mahlon and Chilion married heathen women. That must have grieved Naomi for she could not know how the Lord intended to bless Ruth. Thereupon, it pleased God, besides, to take her two sons from her. That left her a childless widow in a strange country. Only her daughters-in-law were with her, and these were not her people and were not the servants of her God.

Thus Naomi was reduced to the severest extremity. She could not bear to stay in Moab any longer, especially not when she heard that the famine had abated at Bethlehem. Moab was strange and inhospitable to her. Only the graves of her husband and of her two sons were there. In this affliction the only source of her comfort was her daughters-in-law, and the marriage of these had grieved her. Therefore she planned the return to Bethlehem. An unconscious, secret force urged her on, and would not leave her at peace. And, indeed, why stay in Moab? Bethlehem was her native town and all her kinswomen were there. Therefore she determined to return.

She took her way into the hills as an old woman. When she tired she rested herself against the declivities of the hills. Thus, after many a day of hard effort, she reached her dear Bethlehem, the city of her childhood happiness. The inhabitants all observed her closely as she entered the gates. Who could that poor old

woman be? Every feature of her face betrayed lines
of care and bereavement. They could see, of course,
that she was an Israelite, and therefore they ran out
to ask her. In answering, Naomi gave way to tears
and exclaimed with an uprush of Oriental emotion:
"I am Naomi, but call me not Naomi, but call me
Mara, for I am no longer a pleasant woman; I am
sorely wounded at heart. The Almighty hath greatly
afflicted me."

But Naomi did not return alone. One of the two
daughters-in-law, she who was called Ruth, had accompanied her. Naomi had not tried to persuade her.
On the contrary, if the choice had been hers, she would
have left Ruth in Moab, just as she had left Orpah
there. For she thought at the time that, like Orpah,
Ruth still prayed to the gods of Moab. But the Lord
had intervened. Moab had been born of Lot and in
spite of the fact of that terrible sin attached to his origin, yet Lot was justified by God and was one of
Abraham's race. Accordingly, a remnant of faithful
ones remained in Moab. Without Naomi's knowledge,
Ruth was one of these. Therefore the Lord had approached her soul with His omnipotent grace. Thus
Ruth had shifted her allegiance from the gods of Moab
to God, the Lord of Israel. Therefore she had accompanied her mother-in-law because she, too, could not
stay in Moab any longer.

After that Naomi devoted all of her love to that
child. She was poor for she had to live from the
gleanings of the fields. But she planned diligently in
order that at her death Ruth might not be left hope-
lessly behind. She went about those plans in a different way than we should do today. In these mat-

ters she followed the customs of Bethlehem and of her time. She proceeded with tenderness, with calm deliberation, and with a firm trust in the Lord. She was neither haughty nor cowardly. She thought clearly and logically and when she spoke it was with eloquence and preciseness that her words fell from her mouth. Her concern was never with herself but always with the child to whom the Lord had attached her. Thus Naomi subdued bitterness, and her former pleasantness, entirely purged now, returned to her.

God honored that forgotten woman in exceptional ways. He included the account of her life in the Holy Scriptures. He gave her the sympathy of the Church of all ages. But what is chiefly important is that He caused her blood to mingle with that which the Son of God took into His human heart and which was poured at Golgotha for the salvation of the world.

Suggested Questions for Study and Discussion

1. What does the name Naomi mean?
2. Was Naomi a woman of faith?
3. How did God finally bless Naomi?

ORPAH

Behold, thy sister-in-law is gone back unto her people and unto her gods: return thou after thy sister-in-law.—RUTH 1:15

READ — RUTH 1

ORPAH represents a woman to whom grace was extended, who rejected it, and sank back into condemnation. She had come into very close contact with grace. God had directed matters so that because of a famine a family of Israel had fled to her community. Thus Orpah had been permitted to know four people who worshiped the One True God. It was the same God to Whom her forefather Lot had bowed his knees, the same Who had strikingly avenged Himself at Sodom and Gomorrah, and Who had miraculously saved those who accepted Him. Orpah belonged to the generations of Lot's wife as well. And the story, doubtless, was still current in Moab of how God had petrified her because of her unbelief. Now she again heard of these miraculous deeds of the God of Israel. She gained the love of one of Naomi's sons. She could hardly, therefore, have come into closer contact with a true knowledge of God. Four missionaries had come to her at one time from Bethlehem. She had constantly associated with these, and had finally married into the family.

Besides, there was the fact that she had not married alone. Ruth, another Moabitess, had also been given one of Naomi's sons as a husband. And this Ruth illustrated to her how a woman who is alien to the faith ought to permit herself to be mastered by it when once she comes into contact with it. In spite of these invaluable advantages, however, Orpah closed her heart to the saving grace that was extended to her. Moloch had always been her god, and by continuing to embrace Moloch she permitted her soul to be eternally lost.

It is most unlikely that as a married woman she made it a point to ostentatiously oppose the Lord. Inasmuch as Naomi said that she "went back" to her gods, it may be inferred that she had made a virtue of necessity in Naomi's family and had formally acquiesced in the worship of Jehovah. But that conversion to the Lord was purely a formal matter. In her mind marriage was the important thing and religion secondary and incidental. Observe, for instance, what great pains Naomi took to assure her that never again she could receive a husband from the womb of her mother-in-law. This leads us to think that she had, as far as appearances went, emulated her husband's wishes in religious matters. The truth is that Orpah had wanted to marry. And, if her husband had lived, and had given her reasonable prospects for a happy and prosperous life, Orpah would most likely have accompanied him to Bethlehem. There she would have swelled the number of apparent believers.

But the Lord dealt differently with her. Just as He had Ruth's, so He permitted Orpah's husband to die. In this crisis the sincerity of her conversion could be truly tested. Only in this way, to be sure, can we understand the apparent indifference of Naomi to the spiritual welfare of her daughter-in-law. Naomi had often studied Orpah, and had frequently observed that beneath her apparent piety there lurked the unmistakable influence of her former, heathen tendencies. Therefore, Naomi correctly determined that the matter had to be put to a conclusive test. Orpah might go to Bethlehem only if her choice for Israel's God was born from a sincere conviction.

Orpah failed in that test. She thought highly of that poor, childless old widow, but she thought even more highly of rich and prosperous Moab. Israel's God? What had her service of Him availed her? Elimelech had died; Mahlon had died; and Chilion, too, was dead. Therefore she concluded that to go to Bethlehem was to invite sure privation and disaster. Compared with that God, Moloch, the idol of her people, was to be greatly preferred. Hence, she kissed Naomi farewell, and with that farewell kiss she forever separated herself from the Love of God.

Thus Ruth and Orpah, the two women of Moab, separated. Ruth followed Naomi, went to Bethlehem, and became a mother of the Christ. Orpah bade Naomi farewell, returned to Moab and to Moloch, and thrust herself into everlasting doom.

Suggested Questions for Study and Discussion

1. What is the punishment to those that reject the grace God has shown them?
2. Was Orpah selfish?
3. Was Orpah justified in making the decision she made?

RUTH

For all the city of my people know that thou art a virtuous woman.—RUTH 3:11

READ — RUTH 3

RUTH was by no means a young woman at the time that she married Boaz and gave birth to Obed. She had been married to Mahlon for almost ten years, and had at that time been a widow for a considerable length of time. The people of the East, therefore, regarded her as a woman of mature age. It is because she is always seen beside the aged Naomi that we are inclined to think of her as a young woman.

Ruth had the same heathen background that Orpah had. She was also a member of the degenerated tribe of Moab. She had also come into contact with the sacred influence of Elimelech and his family. Unlike Orpah, however, she opened her heart to grace. Internal grace had preceded the external presentation of it. She was elected of God, and because of that there accrued to her both that inner call and Elimelech's external profferment of it. Men had hungered for bread in Bethlehem in order that Ruth might hunger for the bread of life.

We may not conclude from this, however, that Ruth's choice for Jehovah had been more decisive than Orpah's before the time of their separation. It is quite possible that Orpah seemed to give a much warmer reception to Chilion's faith than Ruth did to Mahlon's. Because it is deeply imbedded in the mines, the finest gold often remains long undiscovered. And in profound natures the sterling qualities of character are not always revealed at once.

Naomi does not give Ruth the slightest indication of preference. She speaks to both in the same tone of voice. In the decisive moment she speaks to Orpah first, as if the more docile Ruth generally followed in wake of Orpah's aggressiveness anyhow. And Naomi does that in spite of the fact that, inasmuch as Ruth's husband was her firstborn Mahlon, she should have been first in the order of seniority.

It often happens that quiet personalities tend to slumber complacently in this way until some event shakes them violently out of their lethargy. That event in Ruth's case was Naomi's proposition that they return to Moab.

The three of them had started on their way together. If no one had said anything they would all, doubtless, have gone on to Bethlehem. But Naomi unexpectedly stops and urges them to return to the gods of their people. Orpah takes the hint and goes. In Ruth, however, the conviction of faith, which has so long been latent, suddenly asserts itself. She independently makes a conclusive decision. She completely and gloriously confesses that she wishes henceforth in life and death to be counted with God's people. "Thy people shall be my people, and thy God my God; Where thou goest, I will go, and where thou diest, I will die, and there will I be buried: The Lord do so to me, and more also, if aught but death part thee and me."

Thus we can see that God used her affection for the poor and desolate Naomi as a means of grace. Naomi is the link with which God has forever bound Ruth to His people and to His Messiah.

There is no overdone spirituality in Ruth, no lean and loveless glorying in abstract spiritual values. She gratefully looks into her pious mother's sad face. She clings to that woman. Her faith in the God of Israel mingles with her love for Naomi. She wants to identify herself with her mother-in-law for life and for death. Beneath that love, however, there lies the firm confession that Naomi's God is also her God. In fact, she confesses that God Himself uprooted her from Moab and transplanted her to the people of Israel.

In this way Ruth's faith burst into the light of day. It took the form of quiet, humble service, and remained untainted by any trace of pride or of spiritual haughtiness. Ruth did not say, "Somebody must take care of that helpless old woman, and I suppose I am the one who ought to do it." She respected Naomi's position as a mother, and desired to be her daughter, and to do as she advised.

Therefore she followed the reapers in the field of Bethlehem in order to provide for her mother and her-self. Because she proceeded in humble obedience, God blessed her. Under His direction she chanced to enter the fields of Boaz. Everybody favored her. She was not sent away, but was encouraged and assisted. Then, when Naomi heard of Boaz she wondered whether as her kinsman, he might not marry Ruth. In this matter Ruth again completely accommodated herself to her mother's wishes. In everything, even the boldest, she exercised complete obedience. Thus God wove the thread of her life more intricately into the web of the history of His people.

Boaz married Ruth. Ruth bore him Obed. To Obed Jesse is later born. Thus Ruth, the Moabitess, was included among the elect. She became the mother of David and in this way the mother of Emmanuel, the Saviour of her soul.

Suggested Questions for Study and Discussion

1. Why did Ruth cling to Naomi?
2. How did Ruth reveal a better character than Orpah?
3. How did God particularly bless Ruth?

HANNAH

The Lord maketh poor, and maketh rich; He bringeth low and raiseth up.—I SAMUEL 2:7

READ — I SAMUEL 1

HANNAH became a mother by faith. She first ap-pears as a childless woman. Then she became a mother, and with that her role was completed. After that her name is not once mentioned. Thenceforth, God's revelation is no longer expressed in Hannah, the mother, but in Samuel, the child she besought of the Lord.

In some ways, therefore, Hannah reminds us of Sarah, but there are others in which she is strikingly different. Sarah's love, it is true, also conflicted with that of another woman before she became a mother. But before that child is born to her, we can trace no sign of faith in Sarah. She often laughs in her unbelief, and it is Abraham's firm faith which first induces his wife to believe.

It cannot be said of Hannah that an inspiring influence was exercised upon her by her husband, Elkanah. He was a good man. Each year he religiously went to Shiloh to worship at the Sanctuary. He loved Hannah more than Peninnah, and at public festivities he accorded the higher honors to his dearer wife. It was perfectly obvious to him that Hannah wept because of her barrenness. His question, "Hannah, why weepest thou; am I not better to thee than ten sons?" betrays a truly sympathetic nature. But Elkanah did not have an outspoken, decisive faith. We do not mean to say by that that he was not one of God's elect. But, be it ever so reluctantly, he resigned himself easily to Hannah's childless condition. He never once wrestled in prayer with God, as Abraham did in asking a child of the Lord. It may be that he occasionally inserted into his personal prayers the petition, "Lord, give Hannah my wife, a dear child." But such general prayers do not imply the strenuous conflict of faith which a deeply affected soul demands. Those who pray such prayers feel that nothing is wanting, even

though they remain unanswered. They are not char-
acterized by intense faith.

On the other hand, Hannah had exactly what Elkanah lacked. In the home of a patriarch the husband leads and the wife follows. In Elkanah's home
the situation is reversed, and faith's rivalry is most
hotly waged in Hannah's heart. Barrenness is always
thwarting to a woman who has been married for a
number of years. Many tears are still being shed because of that. But our day understands less clearly
than Hannah did that it is the Lord Who causes
sterility, and that only He can alter that condition.
He does that with a physician's assistance sometimes,
and sometimes without, but in either case it is the
Lord Who controls the conception of children. Our
generation has fallen below the spiritual level which
can appreciate such concepts as that. Instead of looking to God for alleviation of the condition of barrenness, modernity looks to science for an answer. Man
feels self-sufficient and thinks that he can devise es-
capes from all maladies. Observe, however, how diametrically such humanism is opposed to what Hannah
said as she sang "Talk no more so exceeding proudly:
for the Lord is a God of knowledge." Accordingly,
Hannah's distinctive virtue is her faith. She had not
achieved it herself, but it had been given her by God.
The Lord had planned great things for her. He had
led his people to a crossroad in their history, and at
this juncture Samuel was to be born. The Lord shows
us in Hannah's prolonged disappointment and later
ecstasy that he is preparing for Samuel's coming, be-
forehand.

In her distress Hannah surrendered herself completely to the Lord's confidence. Her firm faith was that only God could convert a woman into a mother. Call it a Divine intuition, therefore, or a Divine presentiment, but something there was which urged Hannah on. She knew no contentment. Under God's direction, even Peninnah's constant teasing served to stimulate acute yearning in her heart. She communicated all of her needs to God. She knew that God was the creator of children. She knew that He would be that for her, if she would make Him her sole Fortress, and never cease praying for a child.

The next time that Elkanah and his wife again went to Shiloh for the usual festivities, Hannah unobtrusively crept into the sanctuary. She secreted herself in an inconspicuous corner, close to the wall. There she prayed fervently, passionately even. She wrestled with God and would not relinquish her hold upon Him until her prayer had been answered. Perhaps that prayer was not quite pure and entirely untainted. Very likely the figure of Peninnah tantalized her. She doubtless yearned to triumph over the woman who had annoyed her so mercilessly. At least, in that way we can understand her song "My mouth is enlarged over mine enemies." We know, too, that she was immediately prepared to dedicate the child to the Lord, should it be granted to her. All these things suggest that she desired intensely to be relieved of the shame of her childlessness.

But that prayer was also prompted by an honest and untainted faith in the fact that God could grant her a child. She saw in God not merely a possible answer to prayer, but a certain answer. Her faith in that certainty induced her to cling tightly to the living God.

Her prayer was answered. The Lord gave her Samuel. It is of course, true that not every mother is prepared to give her child away the moment it is born to her. Through Hannah, however, this thought passes from God to all Christian women. Like Hannah these must acknowledge that God gives children. When that acknowledgment has been made, mothers will be glad to dedicate those children to the Lord Who created them.

Suggested Questions for Study and Discussion

1. What prevalent and good characteristic is revealed to us of Hannah?
2. From whom did she receive this characteristic?
3. How is this a lesson to us? What other lesson does her life teach us?

ICHABOD'S MOTHER

And she named the child Ichabod, saying, The glory is departed from Israel; because the ark of God was taken.—I SAM. 4:21

READ—I SAMUEL 4:19-22

Much that is told us in the Scriptures concerning Ichabod's mother reminds us of what was told us about the mother of Benjamin. Like Rachel, she died in giving birth to her child. Those who stood at Rachel's bedside tried to comfort her by saying "Fear not, for thou shalt have this son also." And those who attended Ichabod's mother said "Fear not, for thou hast born a son." Just as Rachel had cried in death's agony, "Name my child Ben-oni," so this woman exclaimed with her final gasps, "Call my child Ichabod, for the glory is departed from Israel."

The parallelisms between these two women strike our attention forcibly. But it would be quite incorrect to think of the two women in the same way. The story of Ichabod's mother is the more touching of the two, for she died a martyr to her firm faith. The Holy Scriptures specifically tell us that. The pains of travail seized her somewhat prematurely when she heard that the ark of the Lord had been lost.

We do not mean to say that her martyrdom to the faith is the sole reason for which this account has been included in the Bible. That were an unwarranted conclusion. Our holy God has a profound sympathy for a mother who is compelled to sacrifice her own life for the sake of the child she is giving the world. He manifests that sympathy by repeatedly calling our attention in the Scriptures to this dark page in the somber history of humanity. We have all known mothers who have sacrificed their lives in this pathetic way. It is probable that some of the daughters in our home whose gleeful laughter now cheers us, are to meet a similar fate. Perhaps we are not interested in Rachel or in Ichabod's mother. But we cannot fail to be interested in this touching narrative, because of the mothers we know and because the same experience may prove to be our daughter's fate.

The case of Ichabod's mother is, however, peculiarly significant. She scared, and that fright induced the pains of travail to seize her. But she scared because she believed.

The report of the death of her husband, Phinehas.

had also affected her, just as had that of the aged Eli, her father-in-law. But the Scriptures indicate that these events did not affect her as intensely as did the loss of the ark of God. When she named her child Ichabod, which means "The glory is departed," she was referring not to Eli's death or to Phinehas' but to the catastrophe which had occurred to the ark. She confirms that fact by twice saying "The glory is departed from Israel for the ark of God is taken."

Her reaction to this catastrophe would not have been as acute as this if her faith had not been deeply-rooted, and if the fear of the Lord had not been her primary interest. We know that Eli also scared when he heard of the news, but Eli's horror was less the result of his faith than of the searching accusation of his conscience. He was shocked because he knew that as a high-priest he should not have allowed the ark to be taken into battle. Ichabod's mother grieved because she felt that the holiness and honor of God had been profaned. She impresses us, therefore, as having been a sincerely faithful person in a priestly family, part of which was weak and part of which was terribly ungodly.

Her husband, Phinehas, like Hophni, her brother-in-law was a despicable man. He seized for his own purposes what was brought him for purposes of sacrifice. He maltreated the pious people who came to the Tabernacle, as a tyrant might have done. He indulged sacrilegious practices in the tent of the Lord. For that reason it was written of him that he was a "Son of Belial, who knew not God." He treated the Israelites dishonestly and threatened them with force.

These things must have grieved Ichabod's mother.

In her distress she probably found some comfort and support in the aged Eli. Eli believed, but he was a spineless and recessive individual. Most likely, therefore, this ignored and rejected woman was the only person in the house who still embodied a positive and effectual faith. Such women, it seems, are committed to trying experiences in life. To them it must often seem that even God has forgotten. At such times despair threatens to overwhelm them. However, believing women do not despair. In His grace, God gives them a calm assurance. Their courage in life remains unbroken, and they are sometimes found praying for the faithless.

In this way the life of Ichabod's mother wore to a tedious close. She witnessed God's awful judgment upon Phinehas and Hophni. She saw that God's wrath was exercised upon Eli, because of his cowardice and timidity. Besides, she was compelled to sense the catastrophe in the loss of the ark more intensely, perhaps, than any in Israel. It caused her to be delivered of her child. And she died in bearing Ichabod.

She died, but she found more than Eli, and more than the ark with God. What she found was hers eternally. Ichabod lived on alone. Only the memory of a bygone past reminded him of his father and mother. Yet, the mother, who dies as Ichabod's did, gives her child the Father Who is in heaven. Knowing that, she died.

Suggested Questions for Study and Discussion
1. Of whom does this character remind us?
2. In giving birth to her child, why did she say, "The glory is departed from Israel"?
3. What was the reward of her faith?

ABIGAIL

*Now the name of the man was Nabal; and the
name of his wife was Abigail: and she was a woman
of good understanding, and of a beautiful counte-
nance: but the man was churlish and evil in his
doings; and he was of the house of Caleb.*

—I SAM. 25:3

READ—I SAMUEL 25:2-42

It seems that also in bygone times incongruous marriages were sometimes consummated. Perhaps the most
striking example of mis-mated couple is that of Nabal
and Abigail. Except for his wealth, he had everything that was unbecoming to and repulsive in a man.
On the other hand, she was a woman whose equal
is not found in a thousand. She embodied all the
qualities a man could desire for his happiness. We
are told that she was remarkably intelligent and discreet, and that she was very beautiful, besides. And
her conduct and activities tell us that she had a most
appealing character and unwavering faith.

Perhaps you feel inclined to reply that she should
never have married such a foolhardy man as Nabal
was. But you must remember that Leah was not
asked whether or not she cared to marry Jacob. In
those regions, and in the crude customs of that day,
young girls were frequently married without having
had the chance to exercise a personal choice.

Abigail, very likely, never got along very well with
Nabal. Indeed, how could she have harmonized beautifully with such a man? His glory was his money.
He loved nothing so much as to indulge drunken carousals with his men. He was churlishly disposed, and

had not a single noble aspiration. In diametrical opposition to God and His Prophet, he allied himself
against David with Saul's political party. That is evident from the words of his reply to David's messen-
gers "There be many servants now-a-days that break
away every one from his master." Accordingly, these
two people were exact opposites in every respect. She
was discreet and beautiful; he churlish and evil in all
his doings. She gloried in the "bundle of life"; he
gloated over his property. She chose to ally herself
with David, the man after God's own heart; he sided
with Saul, God's own reprobate.

Their unfortunate association continued until David
"came to blows" with Nabal. Together with his little
army of six hundred men, David had taken refuge in
the hills and grottos in the neighborhood of Carmel.
This was the region in which Nabal herded his flock.
As an honest soldier, David had never infringed upon
Nabal's rights. Upon occasion he had even assisted
his herdsmen. It still sometimes happens that these
shepherds will reward such rebels with a gift. David
had, in fact, sent for such a gift after Nabal had
harvested a superfluity of food. David's men came
upon Nabal as he was shearing his sheep.

But Nabal had an intense dislike for David. He
belonged to Saul's party, to those who hated the Lord.
Therefore, he greeted David's men coarsely and vitu-
peratively, and sent them away empty-handed. Naturally, David could not permit such an insult to pass
unchallenged. Had it not been for Abigail's timely
intervention, bloodshed would certainly have ensued.
But the moment Abigail heard what had been going
on, she immediately loaded some asses with an abun-

dance of victuals, and sent her servants ahead with these. Then she herself rode on behind in the hope that her gift would first pacify David's anger. After some hours of riding, she reached his camp, fell down at his feet, and spoke to him in a friendly and appropriate way. Her unusually eloquent and ingratiating words immediately palliated David's wrath. He had sent armed men to Nabal, but he immediately issued a counter-command to check them. He was astonished to learn that such an uncouth blockhead as Nabal was, should have such an ideal wife. Hence, it is not surprising, that he should later himself marry her.

Abigail returned to Nabal. She found him drunk, as usual, and had to allow him to "sleep it out." Then she told him that because he had acted so foolhardily, his life had hung suspended by a delicate thread. Nabal was so severely shocked by this that he was seized by convulsions of which he died ten days later.

David discerned one of God's plans in these events. Michal had been given to another man. Inasmuch as God had directed matters in this way, it seemed to him that Abigail was intended to be his wife. He had her sent for, and she gladly took her five maidservants and came to David's camp. For her resolute courage she gained the noble and lovable David as her husband, instead of the foolhardy Nabal.

Nabal was a veritable Belial, and he will always provoke the profoundest aversion in all who read of him. But Abigail will never be forgotten because of the effective words she spoke to David when she said "Yet a man is risen to pursue thee, and to seek thy soul: but the soul of my lord shall be bound in the bundle

of life with the Lord thy God." May we not believe
that a woman who spoke in this way was also bound
in the bundle of life with God?

Suggested Questions for Study and Discussion

1. What type of marriage was Abigail's?
2. How can you account for this marriage?
3. How does Abigail reveal her faith?

M I C H A L

*Therefore Michal the daughter of Saul had no
child unto the day of her death.*—II SAM. 6:23

READ—I SAMUEL 14:49; 18:17-28; 19:11-17: 25:44;
II SAMUEL 3:12-16; 6:16, 23

Michal was the younger of the two daughters who
were born to Saul by Ahinoam. Her older sister's
name was Merab. Saul hoped that each of these
daughters would assist him in causing David's death
at the hands of the Philistines. David was to give
Saul a hundred foreskins of the Philistines as his
dowry for both Merab and Michal. Naturally, Saul
supposed that David would be killed before the hun-
dredth Philistine had yielded his life.

Princess Michal was a woman who gave expression
to her feelings. She was by no means impervious to
the fervor of infatuation. But her most characteristic
trait was her desire for prestige. She was always
busily plotting for it, and for that she dared to do
things. Michal had been deeply impressed by the
young man who had killed the giant Goliath. She
grew passionately fond of him and made no attempt
to conceal her love. When Saul sent his assassins to

kill David, she quickly devised a means to deceive her father's emissaries. She placed an idol in David's bed. Soon after that incident, however, her ardor for David waned. Phalti, she thought, was making a better bid for royalty than he, and she would do anything to secure and hold the glamor of royalty. She knew how to charm men. She succeeded so well in Phalti's case that when she later left him in favor of greater glamor, he followed on behind, weeping all the way. But Michal did not weep. Personal pride and the love of prestige leaves no room for these emotions. David had in the meantime been crowned a king and had expressed a willingness to have her again as his wife. Why should not such a woman as Michal was, leave Phalti in the lurch, then, and go to reign as a queen in Hebron?

Naturally, she could never have become David's ideal love. The things that motivated and inspired each were simply too different. It is true that David had pronounced weaknesses and that he occasionally fell into terrible sins. In spite of these occasional overt actions, however, David was a man who lived for more than himself. The service of God was essentially the highest ideal of his life. He did not become proud of himself when he was made a king. Listen, for instance, to his petition in the nineteenth Psalm: "Keep back thy servant also from presumptuous sins; let them not have dominion over me: then shall I be upright, and I shall be innocent from the great transgression." David knew that pride was the devil's own peculiar vice, and he sensed profoundly the fatal consequences of it.

Michal did not. As a Jewess, she had, perhaps,

prayed to the Covenant God. But we know that she persevered in idolatrous practices from the fact that she kept an image in her house. Hence, she was not in the least affected by the fact that the ark of God was returning to Moriah. David certainly was elated by that event. He was so exhilarated by it that he joined the others as they sacredly danced before it. He was happy, not because it involved personal profit, but because God's honor was restored. Michal's reaction was quite different. She stayed at home and watched the excitement of the throng from her window. She felt that it would hurt her queenly dignity to mingle with the common people. When she noticed that King David participated in the ovation as hilariously as any, and that he joined the daughters of Jerusalem's rabble as they danced their glee before the ark, she felt that she had been poignantly insulted. Why, it was a flagrant breach of etiquette, and, just as it would be to any woman who had no appreciation of essential virtues, a breach of etiquette was as terrible a violation as any Michal could conceive of. In response to her reprimand, David firmly told her the truth. He voiced a judgment of the Lord. God never blessed her with the gift of a child.

Merab bore five sons. David was given many sons and daughters. But Michal was selfish and self-centered; she was proud and fanatically eager for pseudo-prestige. And Michal bore no children until the day of her death.

Because of her indifference to the holiness and perfection of love, Michal was singularly fitted to play the role that she did. She could charm David and Phalti in turn. She caused the simple to stare as she moved about in glistening splendor. But she never achieved the greater attainment of being a mother appropriately.

David's life was devoted to the service of God and to that of his subjects. Saul used a helpless Israel as the means to glorify his own person. Michal embodied that same spirit. She supposed that David should have made it his whole duty to increase her queenly splendor.

Suggested Questions for Study and Discussion

1. What was Michal's trait of weakness?
2. How did God punish Michal for her sin?
3. Why did not Michal enjoy the return of Jehovah's ark?

BATHSHEBA

And David sent and enquired after this woman. And one said, Is not this Bathsheba, the daughter of Eliam, the wife of Uriah the Hittite?—II SAM. 11:3

READ—II SAMUEL 11:2-5, 26, 27; 12:15-24; I KINGS 1: 11-40

IT IS IN connection with Bathsheba's name that we are reminded of David's shocking sin. That sin was of such a horrible and repulsive character, that we loathe even yet to be compelled to associate it with the "man after God's own heart." It represented three distinct transgressions. In the first place, it was an act of ignominious adultery. Secondly, David intoxicated Uriah in an effort to conceal his own guilt in the matter. Finally, when this artifice failed, he deliberately had that innocent and faithful officer of his army murdered.

If the Scriptures had been written to magnify human dignity instead of to praise God's mercy, the account of this unparalleled outrage would never have been included in the chronicles of the kings of Israel. The fact that it is included, on the other hand, constitutes the strongest evidence for the fact that the Scriptures have a Divine origin.

God is not a respecter of the names and of the rank of individuals. He asks us all to take a warning from David's disgraceful conduct. We are all loath to see such palpable wickedness obtruded upon the sacred lineage of the Christ. Besides, this account of David's experience tells each of us that even our most blasphemous sins are insignificant in comparison with the mercies of God.

However, there is profit in observing Bathsheba as well as in studying David. Usually only David is mentioned in connection with this affair. Nothing is said of Bathsheba. Yet, enough is told us about her character to justify us in passing judgment upon her conduct.

The first thing which challenges our attention is her reckless, almost salacious carelessness. It is unbecoming to a woman to take a bath when men are there to see. It cannot be argued that Bathsheba could not have known that she would be seen upon the roof. That excuse might hold if Jerusalem's houses had resembled those in our cities and villages. Our houses have gables and do not serve as a retreat to the inmates of our homes. But in Jerusalem all the houses at that time had flat roofs, which were joined to the substructure by a stairway. It was a fixed custom

among the inhabitants of Jerusalem to refresh themselves upon these roofs in the cool, evening air.

Bathsheba might, therefore, have known, and as a
modest woman she should have made it a point to
know, that she could be seen from the roof of the ad-
joining palace. It may be that she had not detected
David upon the adjacent roof. If she had, it would
have added immeasurably to her sin. Irrespective of
that, however, she undressed, presented herself nudely,
and bathed in a place where she could be seen by anyone upon an adjacent house.

Because of that carelessness we have a low opinion
of Bathsheba's modesty. If she had been appropriately
modest, David would not have been tempted, and the
Anointed of Israel would never have become guilty
of such an outrageous disgrace. What has been said
does not, however, represent the whole of her sin.
She should never have assented to come when David
sent for her. It may be supposed that she had no presentiment of the reason for the summons. Even then,
in the king's palace, and in his bedchamber, she should
have wrestled to death, rather than to have yielded
to adultery. Beyond doubt, therefore, Bathsheba was
not merely the provocation of David's sin, but his accomplice as well. Her later conduct confirms that
opinion. When her husband, Uriah, returned to Jerusalem and remained lying before the door of his house,
she made no attempt to see him. She did not charge
the king with rape, and she did not confess her guilt
with tears. She simply remained in her house. It is
true that when the news of Uriah's death reached
Jerusalem, she observed a formal period of mourning
for him. Thereupon, she immediately went to live at

the palace. She supplemented David's many wives.
And all these events moved so swiftly that she was
already in the palace at the time that she gave birth
to the child she conceived in sin.

The Scriptures do not tell us whether or not she
later grieved because of her conduct, as David did.
It almost seems as if the accusing finger is pointed
at David alone. Hence, the shattered heart and the
sincere repentance of a later day become that much
more clearly manifest. It would be culpable in anyone, of course, to try to diminish David's guilt in the
matter. But the account in the Scriptures also demands that we think of Bathsheba as co-responsible
in David's sin. She serves as a warning to all who,
like her, have been blessed with great physical beauty.
Their creator urges these to walk honorably and mod-
estly before the face of God.

Suggested Questions for Study and Discussion

1. How does a study of Bathsheba reveal God's
   mercy?
2. What first precaution did Bathsheba neglect? Can
   we apply this to our own lives?
3. Are we just in laying the whole guilt of the sin
   on David? Or was Bathsheba co-responsible?

THE WOMAN OF TEKOAH

*And Joab sent to Tekoah, and fetched thence a
wise woman.*—II Sam. 14:2

READ—II Samuel 14:1-22

THE woman whom Joab sent to David to obtain
Absalom's exoneration was an actress. The Bible speaks

of her as a wise woman, but that characterization does not mean that she was wise in the same way as that in which we think of Solomon as having been a wise man. It means that she was worldly-wise, that she could play any assigned role with readiness. Joab know about her, for she lived about as far from Jerusalem as Holland is from Grand Rapids. Hence, it need not surprise us, that he employed her to assist him in his scheme to change David's mind.

Absalom had been exiled from Jerusalem because he had killed Amnon, Tamar's vile seducer. Amnon's act was horribly disgraceful, we know. But Absalom had no right to murder him. David had done the right thing by letting justice take its course even though his own child was involved. It was perfectly just that Absalom should be barred from Jerusalem.

Joab did not like that. Absalom was his hope for Israel's future, after David should have died. Hence, he concocted a scheme which was designed to reopen Jerusalem's gates to the young prince. He persuaded the woman of Tekoah to go to the king, and to employ her art to induce David to restore Absalom to favor. This is what he wished her to do. She was to resort to a device similar to that which the Prophet Nathan had used. Just as Nathan, in the Lord's name, had humiliated David by relating a story of the poor man and his ewe-lamb, so this woman was to influence David by creating a fiction. In her interview with the king, she was to dramatize her story and to impersonate so vividly that David would be induced to respond favorably. Such were her instructions.

She carried them out perfectly. She had exactly understood Joab and he could not have selected a per-

son better qualified to execute his plan. The manner
in which she threw her net over the king was simply
uncanny. She played that she was a widow who had
had two sons. These sons, she said, had quarreled,
come to blows, and one of them had been killed. Now
an avenger was pursuing the murderer. If he should
succeed, she the poor widow, would be left childless
and defenseless. For that reason she was petitioning
the king to intervene in her favor, and to protect her
child.

That was the role she played. And how master-
fully she executed it! Her grief seemed so real that
it touched and stirred the emotions. She set her fate
into such vivid relief that it did indeed seem worthy
of consideration. Notice her consummate ease and
poise as she stood before the king. From the corner
of her eye she tested the effects of her words, and
proceeded to adapt her approaches to David's emo-
tional responses. Now she flattered him, told him that
his wisdom was like an angel's, that he was one
favored of the Lord. Now she sent a shudder through
his body by an allusion to Absalom's fate. Indeed,
on the stage this woman would have commanded a
fabulous salary. She was an accomplished actress. She
was skilled at suggesting the complete illusion.

When she had made her bow, the king suspected
the artifice that lurked beneath her coming, and asked
"Is not the hand of Joab with thee in all this?" She
knew how to answer that question appropriately, too.
She argued with herself that if David should become
enraged, his wrath ought to be directed toward Joab,
not toward herself. Therefore she said "I have played
this role," or to use her own words, "To fetch about

this form of speech hath thy servant Joab done this thing, and my lord is wise according to the wisdom of an angel of God, to know all things that are in the earth." She knew that this answer would absolve her of all responsibility in the matter, and that it would at the same time flatter David into yielding to Absalom's exoneration. David yielded, and because of that brought a judgment of God upon himself.

If the woman of Tekoah had done all of these things upon her own initiative, her guilt in the matter would have been far less culpable. There is no wrong in using a created story to accomplish noble ends. John Bunyan has illustrated that. Consequently, her guilt arises from the fact that she acted at the suggestion of another. She was not motivated by her own convictions. She had professionally complied with Joab's request. Her sin was that she merely "acted," in the full, connotative sense of the word. She had merely played a role. She wanted to demonstrate that she could fascinate the king by her words, gestures, and intonations. That represents the deceitful and ignoble in her character. She teaches all women who, like her, are gifted with histrionic ability, to beware of the sin that attaches to beautiful but false dramatization. Besides, we must all learn from her to beware of succumbing to the mesmerism of an actress.

Suggested Questions for Study and Discussion

1. In what way was this woman wise?
2. Was Joab justified in sending this woman to David?
3. May we use gifts, as God gave them to her, in that manner?
4. What was David's punishment for succumbing to her acting?

THE WITCH OF ENDOR

Behold, there is a woman who hath a familiar spirit at Endor.—I SAM. 28:7

READ — I SAMUEL 28

The witch of Endor reminds us of the woman of Tekoah. Both stepped out of the occupational spheres common to women. She of Tekoah chose that of intriguing and acting. The witch of Endor identified herself with secret and mysterious powers. Thus both made their living and gained an influence in their community by resorting to unusual spheres of activity. The woman of Tekoah created her own art, planned her own intrigues, and relied upon her own skill at dramatization and speech. The woman of Endor employed quite different means. She was not a particularly striking personality. She was hardly an artist; she said nothing extraordinarily significant. She borrowed her resources not from herself, nor from the Lord her God, but from demons and from the mysterious forces of nature.

Women seem to be more susceptible to occult and supernatural influences than men. In man, reason is highly developed, and it displays itself in his character. Hence, we notice that the most successful stage artists and conjurers have been women. We hear very little today about diviners and magicians, but there are still women who practice sorcery and fortune-telling. Women, who take no delight in the true feminine urges and aspirations, are by nature dangerously susceptible to these occult influences, and are inclined to lend sensitive ears to the language of demons. That inclination is owing to their delicate sensibilities, to their pronounced emotions, and to their comparatively weak self-reliance. Satan knew that in Paradise. He approached Adam through the more pliable Eve.

It cannot be said that the woman of Endor had a perverse and despicable character. She still embodied desirably natural, feminine virtues at the time that Saul visited her. We remember that Saul fell prostrate upon the ground when he was told the awful prophecy of his fate. That incident occasioned an expression of many noble, womanly traits in the witch of Endor. She tried to assist and comfort him. She had his servants lay him upon her own bed. She insisted that he eat, and when he finally assented, she took her fatted calf and prepared an abundant meal for Saul and his servants. Before these demonstrations of sympathy, too, she had said nothing immodest or unbecoming to a woman. She made no attempt to make a glamorous and lasting impression. There was no attempt to hide deceit behind a curtain of impressive hokus-pokus.

Just that last characteristic, of course, betrays how completely she had surrendered herself to sin. It is a terrible sin to try to make obvious deceit appear to be true by a gamut of illusions and tricks. But the witch of Endor did not deceive. She seems actually to have communicated with demons. And this sin is far profounder than the former.

We repeatedly read in the Scriptures of all kinds of wizards, diviners, soothsayers, jugglers, conjurers, and sorcerers. These indulged in occult practices and exerted a great influence in Babylon Egypt, Moab, and among the Philistines. And the influence of those who sought and seek their strength in the powers of darkness has continued through the centuries to the present day. God has forbidden communication with demons, but, in spite of His command, there have been those everywhere who continue to indulge it. The witch of Endor was one of these. She had become prominent because of her practice. Saul himself had commanded that all sorcerers should be killed. But this woman had become so well known in spite of this, that, when Saul asked for a woman who had a familiar spirit even his court officials could immediately point her out.

The phenomenon of witchcraft merely confirms the fact that God has created souls in us which are susceptible to influences from above. By this capacity we can borrow strength from God and express it in the influence of faith. But sinful men have turned this God-given capacity to uses diametrically opposed to those the Creator intended. He uses it to communicate with forces from below and to exert an influence in favor of Satan against God.

Who can say what levels of spiritual achievement the witch of Endor might not have attained if she had surrendered to God instead of to Satan. She might have found redemption with him Who alone could have saved her from evil. Instead she sold herself to Satan.

Her type has not entirely disappeared. One reluctantly observes that her kind can still be found in Christian countries. Cheap fortune-tellers and magicians are still making money by the means which she employed. That represents an awful sin in those who practice it, and in those who consult and pay for it.

Suggested Questions for Study and Discussion

1. What does this meditation teach concerning the divinely instituted place of woman?
2. Was it Biblical for Saul to visit a witch?
3. Was her revelation from God or the devil?
4. May we as Christians have our fortunes told (using the common phraseology)?

THE PEASANT WOMAN OF BAHURIM

And the woman took and spread a covering over the well's mouth, and spread ground corn thereon, and the thing was not known.—II SAM. 17:19

READ—II SAMUEL 17:18-21

In a crucial moment a woman of Bahurim, a village near Jerusalem, saved David's life, David's army, David's kingdom, and, if you choose, saved the future of Israel and of God's Kingdom.

Absalom had rebelled against his father. David had been compelled to flee from his own son. And Ahithophel was a designing man who was bent on David's destruction. Everything depended upon whether or not David could retain communication with Jerusalem, upon whether or not he could remain conversant with Absalom's plans. Only in that way could he and his small group of men hope to escape from Absalom's much larger army.

This was the situation. David had stationed two of his most faithful servants at the well of Enrogel. He had arranged with Hushai, his friend, who had remained at Jerusalem, that he should send a message to the men at that well, and thus keep him acquainted with the situation at Jerusalem. In order to avoid all suspicion, Hushai had selected one of his maid-servants instead of a man to be his emissary to En-rogel. She left Jerusalem's gates inconspicuously, and, looking as innocent as she could, she went to the well. There she gave Jonathan and Ahimaaz the indispens-able information which alone could save David's army from complete annihilation.

But this strategy failed. Naturally, close watch was being kept from every wall and watch-tower, lest any communication should reach David from his friends at Jerusalem. A young soldier detected that maid-servant, kept a close eye upon her, observed that she had spoken to two men at Enrogel, and that those two men had thereupon hastily run away. He sounded the alarm. Jerusalem's gates were opened to a troop of Absalom's fastest runners, and these started in pur-suit of their enemies.

Everything, therefore, hung suspended by a very frail thread. If Jonathan and Ahimaaz had been over-taken, no information would have reached David from Jerusalem. Then Absalom would have succeeded in unexpectedly pouncing upon David's handful of sol-diers in unprotected country. Judging by human stan-dards, David's army would in that event have been completely routed, and Absalom would not have hesi-tated to take his father's life.

But this is what actually happened. Jonathan and Ahimaaz happened to look back and they noticed that they were being pursued. They ran as fast as they could but in a long run they could impossibly have escaped their pursuers. Thus they came to the village of Bahurim and noticed a garden in their way in which there was an empty well. As it seemed to them, noth-

ing better could be done than to conceal themselves
in that well before those who pursued them should
arrive. But that would have availed them nothing,
for it could be easily seen from the road that they
were concealed in the pit. They would most certainly
have been detected and captured if David had not had
unknown friends in that village, and if a woman of
Bahurim had not been devoted to David's cause with
her whole heart and soul.

It happened that the garden in which the well was
located belonged to a man whose wife was as faithful
to David's cause as she was handy in her actions. She
had seen, perhaps through her window, that those two
men had come running down the road and that they
had jumped into the pit. She understood at a glance
what it was all about, and sensed immediately that
those men had to be saved. She knew that they would
meet with certain death if they were to stay in the
well as it was. Her actions were as rapid as her
thought. In less than no time she seized a cloth from
her house and covered the mouth of the well with it.
Then she snatched a basket of corn from her doorway
and spread it over the cloth. Nothing could then be
seen of the pit, and to all appearance there was merely
a heap of corn, drying in the sun.

Then, before the runners arrived, she ran to the
gate of the yard, and nonchalantly awaited their coming. Sure enough! They stopped a moment to ask if
she had seen two men running past that way. In a
twinkling of an eye she had replied that they had long
gone on their way. Thus she diverted the pursuers'
course in a wrong direction, so that these had, after
a time, to give up in defeat, and to return to Jeru-

salem empty-handed. In this way David's life was saved.

The Lord achieved this thing. He directed matters so that Jonathan and Ahimaaz detected that particular well in that particular garden. He had done that because he knew that it was owned by a woman who was devoted to David's cause. He planned that that woman should be there at that moment, and that she should see what was going on. He saved her from becoming "rattled" in those exciting moments, and enabled her to work energetically and skillfully to the end. And He prevented her face from betraying any tremor which might have excited any suspicion.

Very likely David had never before heard of or seen that woman. She was one of those inconspicuously faithful ones, whom the Lord had attached to David's cause. She must have been a quiet prayerful woman, who had prayed especially frequent since David's exile. And this woman was chosen by God to induce Absalom's runners to follow a blind trail. She was chosen to save the life of her king, and to thwart Absalom's strategy against David.

In great movements the strength of a hero is not always found among his mighty friends and allies. A simple peasant woman was selected in a crucial moment to save David's whole cause, and thus, to save the cause of God's kingdom.

Suggested Questions for Study and Discussion

1. How did God save David and his cause?
2. Does God use inconspicuous people to attain His end? If so, isn't there a place for us in His work now? Mention some things we can do.
3. Is a lie ever justifiable?

THE REAL MOTHER OF THE
ILLEGITIMATE CHILD

*Then the king answered and said, Give her the
living child and in no wise slay it: she is the mother
thereof.*—I KINGS 3:27

READ — I KINGS 3: 16-28

WE shall not at this point focus our attention upon
Solomon's verdict, but shall instead center it entirely
upon the two women depicted by the Scriptures in relation to it. It is the intent of the Scriptures that we
study them not merely at plaintiffs at court, but that
we also observe their character as women.

Every human heart has praised Solomon for his
just and wise decision in his suit at law. But each of
us should rejoice as well because of the noble material
affection which the real mother of the living child displayed, in spite of her previous reprehensible conduct,
when she opposed Solomon's first proposition. She had
been a wicked woman; she had reveled in sin; had
induced another woman to join her in her illicit practices; and had profaned the city of God by having set
up a public house of prostitution in one of its byways
or alleys. To this extent she is a revolting figure and
causes us to turn away in disgust.

But she also illustrates how even the most degen-
erate can retain a remnant of genuine worth. The
other mother, she who could have enjoyed seeing the
little creature cut in two, was a much baser woman
than she who loved it too much to permit it to be
killed. Compared with the real mother, that first
brutal woman recedes into the dark background. Even
in her, however, there is something that appeals to

us. She wanted another child instead of her dead one, and in this way she hoped to forget that she had unwittingly and accidentally killed her own. And today, in countries where the gospel professedly rules the thought and the conduct of the people, the Christian conscience is wounded time and again by hearing that an unmarried woman has deliberately murdered her own child. In this Christian nation there are daughters who, having yielded to sin, thereupon destroy the children they bore in their bosoms. In this narrative we read of one immoral woman in crude and uncouth Israel who resorted to deceit to get a child, and of another who was willing to make the last splendid sacrifice in order to save her babe.

Solomon could not have placed his proposition before all the women of our Christian civilization. Today, many a woman asks, "How can I be rid of my child?" If she should find that her baby had died during the night through no fault of her own, a load would be lifted from her heart. Present day culture, not the Jerusalem of Solomon's time, is familiar with the gruesome practice, which, although couched in beautiful terms, is nothing less than the base murder of innocent and defenseless creatures.

A bitch fights for her whelps when they are attacked, and a hen offers resistance when her chicks are threatened. And there are women, unworthy of the name, who invoke God's eternal wrath upon themselves, who cold-bloodedly murder their own children in an attempt to avoid the shame of guilt. How could Solomon have dared to place his proposition before such as these? He dared too in his day because he thoroughly knew his people, including the harlots among them, and he relied without misgivings upon the fact that natural, maternal instincts had not been extinguished in any in Israel.

We do not mean to say that an expression of maternal affection extraordinarily praises a woman. If it represents nothing more than an external passion to preserve her child, she has nothing more to boast of than any female animal has. In fact, woman is frequently outdone by the animals in the protection of their young. Besides, we know that essentially egotistic women sometimes "dote on their children," and could not be separated from their "darlings" by force. It is a matter of pure instinct. It was expressed in the woman who appeared before Solomon, and is a resplendently beautiful trait created in women by God. Women do not acquire maternal affection. It is given them by their Creator, and He should be praised for it.

In animals this trait remains forever constant in its manifestations. The hens on the streets of Jerusalem flew into a rage when danger threatened. So do those on ours. But women have been placed before a responsible, moral choice. She can ennoble the maternal instinct, or she can extinguish it.

The mother of the living child who appeared before Solomon, illustrates the truth that we have no right to think that a woman has lost her sense of maternal affection simply because she has yielded to sin. We live in an age of culture, but it has taught us that simply because a woman has not surrendered to seduction, she does not for that reason rep esent ideal motherhood. There are those whose conduct in general is quite uncensurable, but who look forward to childbirth with dread. Later, when their child is born, they are eager to submit it to the surveillance of another. On the other hand, there are women whose illicit practices are positively revolting to us, and who give a beautiful and noble expression in their passionate fondness for their children. We must praise them for this.

The real mother of the illegitimate child in Solomon's courtroom was that kind of mother. Irrespective, therefore, of how sinful her conduct was, we must praise her for the maternal affection which she displayed. She not only happened to be a mother; she also proved to be one. Her example flagrantly embarrasses that of many an unworthy mother of our Christian society.

Suggested Questions for Study and Discussion

1. What good is there in each of these two women?
2. What modern application can we learn from this study?
3. What does this Biblical Narrative teach us relative to Birth Control?

RIZPAH

And Rizpah the daughter of Aiah took sackcloth, and spread it for her upon the rock, from the beginning of harvest until water dropped upon them out of heaven, and suffered neither the birds of the air to rest upon them by day, nor the beasts of the field by night.—II SAM. 21:10

READ — II SAMUEL 3:7; 21: 8-14

THROUGHOUT the successive centuries Rizpah has been an attractive figure to all those who know how to appreciate genuinely noble conduct. She gave expression to a deep-seated and unaffected nobility. She was highly respected as one of the more prominent women of Israel, for she had gone to serve as a concubine in Saul's harem. We read nowhere that she arrogated a prominent position to herself, but it is recorded that, after Saul's death, she illegitimately yielded to Abner's desire. In this respect there is nothing appealing about her, and much that provokes disgust and betrays feminine weakness. It is in the care that she bestowed upon the corpses of her sons, Armoni and Mephibosheth, and of those of the five sons of Michal's sister, that Rizpah accomplished a most beautiful deed.

This was the situation. Saul, whose arch-sin ever and anon was pride, had broken an oath which had been made to the Gibeonites. You perhaps remember who the Gibeonites were. They belonged to the Amorites. They were the people who tried to give Joshua the impression that they had come from a distance, by approaching him in tattered garments and with mouldy bread. Joshua had thoughtlessly made a treaty with them at that time. Their deceit was, of course, soon detected. But the treaty had been made, the word of honor passed, the oath had been taken, and Joshua had sealed the oath with the Lord's name. Consequently, Gibeon could not be destroyed by the sword. They remained within Israel's domains, and were appointed to serve as hewers of wood and drawers of water. Thus Joshua and Israel demonstrated that an oath taken in the name of the Lord remained binding, even though it had been made to a guilty party. This incident has been included in the Scriptures to assure us that God's promises to us are certain, even though we, as were they of Gibeon, are very sinful. Over against God we are the Gibeonites. If guilt had

served as a justification for Joshua to break his oath
with Gibeon we could not, as sinners, expect the fulfillment of God's promises to us.

Israel had kept their treaty with Gibeon to the let-
ter throughout the years. Then Saul came to the throne.
He felt that his whole duty as a king was to put God's
plans into effect, and he identified God's plans with
his own. It is true that he generally acted with a good
purpose in view. But it is equally true that his own
designs were substituted for God's plans. Because of
mere human sympathy he saved Agag's life. He thought
that as a king he ought to have been the one to offer
sacrifices instead of Samuel, the priest. And he personally concluded that, inasmuch as they constituted
a heathen settlement in a holy land, the Gibeonites
ought to be destroyed. He did not entirely annihilate
them, but he completely routed them, and by that act
the oath which Joshua had taken in their behalf was
broken. The promise which Israel had given Gibeon
in God's name was profaned.

That unfaithful act had to be penalized. Saul had
hardly met with death upon Gilboa, before the Gibeonites came to ask compensation in the form of the lives
of seven sons of Saul's family. David had to comply
with that request. He designated the two sons of Rizpah,
Armoni and Mephibosheth, and the five sons of Michal's
sister as the victims of Saul's breach of faith. These
were given to the Gibeonites and were duly hanged
upon the gallows.

At this juncture Rizpah displayed her beautiful nobility. She could not have saved her sons from death.
Both bodies already dangled from the gallows. It had
been inevitable that tragic justice should have pur-

sued them. They had met with a disgraceful death. But a human voice shrieked from the dead bodies, and it called for appropriate respect for the dead. Left unguarded, the hawks and vultures would come and pick the eyes out of the sockets of those corpses and would tear the rotten flesh from the bones. Rizpah knew that that would happen, and that it would be an unnecessary disgrace. Therefore she hastened to the Gibeonites at the peril of her life. These were thirsty for revenge, and might have felt inclined to slake their thirst by taking Rizpah's life also. But she took no thought for herself. Her soul was occupied with the single thought of saving her children from that last disgrace. She spread a cloth of mourning over the rocks that supported the gallows. She placed herself upon that cloth and kept watch over the dead bodies. She sat, she stood, she wrestled with sleep through anxious days and more anxious nights. Weeks became months. And she kept her awful vigil from the time of the early harvest to the season of the late rains. Her heart quivered at the approach of the vulture at night, but by her wild cries and gestures she drove the robber away. The foul stench of her own sons' rotting bodies assailed her nostrils, but she learned to persevere in spite of that worst of obstacles. Her sleep was a semi-waking for she remained always alert to the first clatter of the approaching vulture's wings.

Thus she fulfilled her duty to her children and beautified her motherhood. She protected the corpses. No bird of prey desecrated them. The human tenderness of this woman at those brutal gallows still moves all who read this touching narrative today. She gave

expression to a true and profound nobility. That is
the legitimate praise that accrues to anyone who, like
Rizpah, does a thing without the hope of reward, under
circumstances in which nothing can be personally
gained and in which much can be lost, and who is motivated by a good and noble purpose. David appreciated her act. When he heard of her impressive vigil,
he ordered that the bodies be taken down, and that
the skeletons be buried with those of Saul and Jonathan. In this way Rizpah's passionately fervent prayer
for a proper respect to her dead was answered by
the Lord.

Suggested Questions for Study and Discussion

1. How can we learn from this study that God's
   promises are true?
2. What is the beautiful trait of Rizpah?
3. Were her actions rewarded?

JOB'S WIFE

*Then said his wife unto him, Dost thou still retain
thine integrity? Curse God, and die.*—JOB 2:9

READ — JOB 2: 1-10

IT IS doubtful whether anyone was ever placed before a severer trial than was Job. God allowed Satan
to take everything away from him that could possibly
have been a source of encouragement to him. And
when Satan had robbed him of all these things, he
permitted him to keep what most grieved him. Satan
permitted Job's wife to live. If the Devil had supposed that the slightest semblance of comfort might
have been given Job by his wife, he would certainly

have robbed him of her. But Satan knew he could
use her as an instrument with which to grieve and
torture his victim, and for that reason he permitted
her to live. The best commentators have always interpreted Satan's actions and the character of Job's
wife in this way. Long ago, Augustine spoke of her
as the "Devil's accomplice," and Calvin did not hesitate to call her "an instrument of Satan" and a "diabolical fury." Pseudo-gallantry and sentimentality
have attempted to furbish her dull finish, but the at-
tempts have failed. The words she spoke to Job cannot be erased, and the poignant significance of these
cannot be distorted.

Faith's bow had been drawn to the breaking point
in Job's heart. A hairsbreadth of added exertion, it
seemed, would cause it to snap. Job was at the point
of surrendering to Satan. He was tortured by physical pains and tantalized by spiritual griefs. At this
moment his wife visited him as he sat upon the heap
of ashes. She refused to give him the slightest hint
of encouragement. She did not even reveal a token
of ordinary human sympathy. Instead, she diabolically
urged him to relinquish his faith in God and to end
his suffering by suicide.

Whoever is not familiar with the Hebrew language
perhaps misses the full force of what she said. Her
"Curse God, and die" means and can only mean "Bid
God farewell, divorce yourself, emancipate yourself
from Him, and commit suicide." Whoever wishes to
ascertain that this is the exact meaning of her words,
will find confirming evidence by referring to what
Jezebel urged Ahab to do with Naboth (I Kings
21:10). We read there that Ahab was to appoint two

sons of Belial to serve as witnesses against Naboth.
These were to indict him with having blasphemed God
and the king. As a blasphemer he was then to die
as one guilty of the highest treason. The same word
is used in the Book of Job to designate the type of
offense which Job was urged to commit against the
Most High.*

How terrible! How appalling! Certainly Job's wife
had also been given him as a helpmeet. At this moment Satan's attack upon his victim's soul was so over-
whelming that Job almost succumbed to it. And in
just this moment that diabolical woman rushed to
Satan's assistance. She brutally proposed to her husband that he curse God, sell his soul to Satan, and take
his own life. Surely, no woman could have been less
faithful to her Divine calling than she.

Whoever, henceforth, tries to visualize the suffering of Job, ought to include in his picture, of course,
the bereavement of his children, the loss of his property,
and the irksome charges of his false friends. But he
ought also to include in it the terrible temptation and
the intense grief which his wife occasioned. In her the
last spark of a woman's love, the last reminder of feminine devotion, had been completely extinguished.

For that reason the most gratifying aspect of Job's
tragedy is, perhaps, the scathing but beautifully appropriate answer which he gave his wife. "Thou speak-
est," he retorted from the ashheap, "as one of the

* This paragraph is doubtless occasioned by the possibly
ambiguous meaning of the Dutch word "zegenen," which is the
verb used in both the Book of Job and in that of Kings. The
more specific connotation of the English verb "curse" in the
first book and "blaspheme" in the second obviates the am-
biguity and really renders this paragraph superfluous.—The
Translator.

foolish women. What? Shall we receive good from
the Lord, and shall we not receive evil?"

In our Christianized society women seldom display
the diabolical traits of character in Job's wife as flagrantly as she did. They do not provoke their husbands to curse God in as outspoken a manner. They
do not urge him to commit suicide. Our age dislikes
clearly defined distinctions, and does not choose conclusively for or against God. This generation has em-
braced a number of midway positions, a group of con-
fused boundaries. Thus, modern civilization tends to
confuse the sharp antithesis between a choice for God
and a choice for Satan.

But there are still women who tend to keep their
husbands from firmly fixing their faith in God. They
obstruct an outspoken and courageous zeal for the
Lord. They detain him at Bethel, when his destiny
is Jerusalem. Nonetheless, women have a delicate and
beautiful responsibility in marriage. When everything
that binds their husbands to God and their Saviour
vanishes, they must persist in encouraging him, must
wrestle with Satan for their souls, must draw them
back to their Saviour by the bonds of persevering love.
God has given women an affectionate heart, a mild
disposition, and a sensitive love, in order to qualify
them for that. Yet it frequently occurs that they do
the exact opposite. We see men who are still firm in
their faith in God. Beside them are wives whose
hearts are selfish and wilful, and who try to wrench
religion out of shape and into a thousand twists and
folds. Then they interject their selfish hearts and
their distorted religion between their husbands and their

Saviour. Thus they became guilty of the sin that cursed
Job's wife.

Suggested Questions for Study and Discussion

1. Did Job's wife fulfill her divine calling?
2. Did Job's wife assist and encourage him by her
   words?
3. What should she have done?

THE QUEEN OF SHEBA

*The queen of the south shall rise up in judgment
with this generation, and shall condemn it: for she
came from the uttermost parts of the earth to hear
the wisdom of Solomon; and, behold, a greater than
Solomon is here.*—MATT. 12:42

READ — I KINGS 10: 1-13; MATTHEW 12:42

IT IS nowhere written that the Queen of Sheba was
a converted heathen woman. In fact, there is enough
written to induce us to believe that she was not converted. Had she been called of the Lord, her first concern upon entering Jerusalem would have been to go
to the Holy Temple to offer sacrifices to the God of
Israel. But we are not told that she did so in either
the account that is given in I Kings 10, or in the narrative of II Chronicles 9. We read that she came to
Jerusalem, that she came to see everything that was
resplendently and gorgeously beautiful in Solomon's
palaces and gallaries, and to hear the wisdom of the
king. But there is not a single word which suggests
that she had identified herself with the true religion,
or that she had even enquired about it.

It is true that she exclaimed at the end of her visit,

"Blessed be the Lord thy God, which delighted in thee, to set thee on the throne of Israel." But a heathen person would naturally speak in that way. He believes that there are many gods, and therefore finds it easy to acknowledge that that other God, Whom Israel serves, also exists. And we must note that the Queen of Sheba specifically said "The Lord thy God." In this way she distinguished between Solomon's God and her own.

We have no more reason to infer from Jesus' statement that this queen had been converted from the worship of idols to that of Israel's God. Jesus also said that they of Nineveh should rise up in the day of judgment against His generation. And on another occasion He affirmed that those of Sodom and Gomorrah should witness against the people of His day. Hence, when Jesus said "The queen of the south shall rise up in judgment against this generation, and shall condemn it, for she came . . . to hear the wisdom of Solomon" He meant that in one specific characteristic only the Queen of Sheba was superior to the generation with which He wrestled.

The narrative makes perfectly obvious what that characteristic was. Sheba's Queen was a woman who had avoided the sin of indifference. Things mattered to her. Her interests were wide and varied. She was interested not merely in beautiful clothes and gorgeous finery, but she was also an eager student of that which adorns the mind. She had heard that a wonderful king had ascended the throne of Israel. She had heard that his wisdom and profundity had surpassed that of every sage in his country; that he had not always possessed this rich culture, but that it had been bestowed upon him in an unusual way. And when she heard

that, she could not rest until she had shared in it.
She, too, was by no means a stupid woman. She had
devoted herself to the arts and sciences to such an
extent that she felt quite unembarrassed by the pros-
pect of engaging Solomon in a profound discussion.
She wanted to debate with him, and in this way to put
his wisdom to a searching test.

She was willing, even, to sacrifice much for this
visit and interview. It meant that she had to take a
long journey which involved more time than is at present required to encircle the world. It involved the
expenditure of a considerable amount of money. There
were traveling expenses to be paid, and she felt it
obligatory, besides, to take precious gifts with her to
Solomon's court. But such considerations did not deter
her from going. She understood that a woman, too,
had been appointed to higher things than to merely
dispose of daily, domestic duties. Therefore she under-
took the journey.

She came to Jerusalem. She heard Solomon. She
saw his glory. She was ravished intellectually by hearing him, and was aesthetically thrilled by the taste-
fully selected luxury at his court. And that was all.

The Queen of Sheba was not much different from
many of the young women of the higher classes among
us today. They are eager to know everything. They
have highly developed tastes, and can appreciate the
beautiful, especially the artistically beautiful. They
make it a point to enjoy the cultural attainments of
every country. This is a precious and praiseworthy
pursuit, and implies that they are not afraid of rigorous discipline. They are superior to those who are
indifferent, and to those who embrace the "What do

I care?" attitude of the culturally mediocre. They reveal a desirably alert and interesting spirit, and they are fond of inquiry. Had they lived in Solomon's day, they would certainly have made a trip to Jerusalem, just as they now travel to Paris and London, to Vienna and Berlin. Such women are by no means the avowed enemies of faith. They like the poetry of religion. Doubtless, they would have marveled in breath-taking bewonderment at the external beauty of the Temple at Jerusalem.

But they forget one thing. They forget that a greater than Solomon is here. They forget that that greater One does not primarily ask them to appreciate the beauty of His word, but that he asks them for the surrender of their hearts, and for a complete consecration to His service. Unfortunately, few of these refined young women ever reach that point. They are willing to participate in religion for culture's sake. Jesus may even be a somewhat greater man to them than Solomon was. But they do not regard Him as the Redeemer of their sin and guilt. Consequently, they do not feel intimately attached to Him, nor inclined to praise Him gratefully. For that reason these interesting and interested young women remain at the stage which the Queen of Sheba reached and go no farther. They come to Jerusalem. They are amazed and awe-struck. And they leave Jerusalem.

Suggested Questions for Study and Discussion

1. Was the Queen a converted woman? How can we conclude this?
2. Was she any different than the present day cultured woman?
3. Why did Christ say that she would condemn the generation of His time?

JEROBOAM'S WIFE

*And Jeroboam said to his wife, Arise, I pray thee,
and disguise thyself, that thou be not known to be
the wife of Jeroboam, and get thee to Shiloh: behold, there is Ahijah the prophet.*—I KINGS 14:2

READ — I KINGS 14: 1-17

THE husband is the head of the wife, but must a
wife for that reason assent to everything her husband
demands of her? The Holy Scriptures give us an
answer to that constantly recurring question in this
account of the conduct of one of the queens of Israel.
That queen was the wife of Jeroboam. He was the
first king to rule over the Ten Tribes. Both Jeroboam
and his wife still partly served Jehovah, but they had
mixed all kinds of false ingredients with the true religion. We know the names of two of their children.
The one was called Abijah and the other Nadab. As
frequently seems to be the case, one of these sons
had inherited all the good tendencies of his parents,
and the other all the evil traits. Abijah became heir
to whatever of the fear of the Lord there still remained in the hearts of his parents, and Nadab embodied all their idolatrous folly. Of Abijah, who died
very young, it is written "in him there is found some
good thing toward the Lord God of Israel" (I Kings
14:13). And of Nadab we read that he "did evil in
the sight of the Lord."

We frequently observe that people who prefer the
easy morality of partly clinging to Jehovah and partly
serving idols, in times of stress begin to grow strikingly
Christian in their conduct. Just so, this king and queen
began to think more seriously of Jehovah the moment

adversity entered their home. Their youngest child became critically ill. Abijah was dying. And Jeroboam suddenly became very pious. He wanted to seek Jehovah's assistance again. This need led his thoughts back to the old prophet, Ahijah, the man who prophesied long before that Jeroboam should become king. He felt that he had to establish contact with that Ahijah. Certainly he would know what fate was awaiting the young crown prince.

But who was to be sent to Ahijah at Shiloh? That question caused Jeroboam considerable consternation. His conscience accused him of having deliberately ignored Ahijah's counsel, when he had persisted in setting up the golden calves. No, if Ahijah were to learn that the sick child was his, his prophecy would be sure to involve death and the grave for his son. Indeed, Ahijah must be consulted, but he must not know that the child was his.

Hence, Jeroboam spoke to his wife. "You know what we will do. You go. Put on ordinary peasant clothes, and take with you a simple present such as a peasant woman might bring. Then Ahijah will not know whose child is involved in this matter, and it may be that he will prophesy life for our son."

His wife should have answered, "Jeroboam, I may not do that. It would be deceiving God's prophet. It would provoke God's wrath and He will wreak His vengeance upon us." But she said nothing, procured the clothes of a peasant woman, and quietly did what her husband commanded her.

She met with a terrible fortune. The Lord told Ahijah of her coming and of her deceit. And this was the Prophet's burden to her. Not only was the child to die, but Jeroboam's whole house was to be destroyed. Her child would have died before she returned to Tirzah, and he would be the last to receive an honorable burial. The rest of Jeroboam's house—Baasha accomplished God's curse upon it—was to be gruesomely murdered.

What do the Scriptures intend to teach us by this episode? That we may not deceive? But that is self-evident. That we may not disguise ourselves? The Scriptures tell us in another place in what circumstance disguises are legitimate and in which they are not. Nothing is said about it in this connection. Instead, they plainly inform us that the chiefest sin of Jeroboam's wife was that she assented to doing her husband's command in spite of the fact that that command was evil in the sight of the Lord.

The extent to which a wife should remain in submission to her husband has its limits. Those boundaries are not fixed by what she approves or does not approve of. If a situation is given in which her will opposes his in a matter, her conception of a situation differs from his, if one or the other must submit, then the wife must yield. But a limit to the extent of her submission, one which may never be transgressed, is that which is determined by her conscience. As often and as soon as a Christian woman, enlightened by God's Word, is assured by her conscience that her husband is demanding a thing of her which is forbidden by God, she may not submit, but must offer resistance, come what may.

Man is endowed with authority and he is responsible to God for it. But that authority has been delegated to him by God, and may for that reason never be used against God Himself. Each time a man abuses his authority he loses it, and it no longer avails him anything. At such times a wife is no longer bound by it. She may not even acknowledge it. And any woman who, as did this queen, at such an instance acquiesces in her husband's sinful designs, no longer serves as a "helpmeet" to him. She condemns him and follows him to condemnation.

Suggested Questions for Study and Discussion

1. Must a wife assent to every demand of her husband? What does the Bible teach?
2. What was the sin of the queen?
3. Why did God punish Jeroboam? How?

THE WIDOW OF ZAREPHATH

Arise, get thee to Zarephath, which belongeth to Zidon, and dwell there: behold, I have commanded a woman there to sustain thee.—I KINGS 17:9

READ — I KINGS 17

WE propose to focus our attention not upon Elijah's miracle but upon the widow of Zarephath.

She had lost her husband, and thus had been deprived of him upon whom she had depended for a livelihood. She had a child who, so far from supporting her, still depended upon her for support. She was, therefore, a woman oppressed by many cares, and one who was to be placed in strait circumstances. That which distinguishes a widow from an unmarried woman is that she had been bereaved of that which enabled her to live a carefree life. She is frequently a mother whose cares exceed her capacity to cope with them. In her widowed state this woman of Zarephath had lost her faith. True, she still most certainly believed in the God of Israel. As a young girl she had probably belonged to a group of eager daughters whose delight was to serve the Lord. At least it is obvious from this narrative that the Lord dealt with her in an unusual way.

But a momentous occurrence had overtaken her now. God had taken the man she loved, the father of her child, from her. She was left desolate and alone in secluded Zarephath. Life was hard. At first she found things possible. She kept up the struggle with fortune. Then the early rains failed, the harvest failed, and the prices of foodstuffs became exhorbitant. Famine stalked through the land. And, just as they do now, such catastrophes most seriously injure those who, in times of prosperity, can just "make ends meet."

It was in this distress that her faith grew weak. Despair gained control of her heart. All grew dark before her eyes, and there was no rift in the darkness, no hope for the future. There was little left to eat, and little to give her child. Especially that broke her heart. Life had become too much for her. But there was still flour and oil enough to prepare one meal. She could do that at least. And then! Then she would throw herself and her son upon the rickety old cot and await the death of her child, and her own release from suffering. Release — but by the awful death of starvation.

However, a stranger came to her in that crucial moment and asked her for a drink of water. Well, there was still water enough. She mechanically fetched a vessel, filled it with water, and gave it to the man.

But he asked for more. He asked for food. Just as if he had come to mock her poverty and her critical need! What? You ask me for bread? Me, a poor widow, who am in despair, because I and my child are at the point of starving to death? Thus she must have reasoned in her mind. And, indeed, it did seem as though he were mocking her dire need.

But God had sent that man, and with him had sent relief. A miracle happened. The flour remained constant and the oil did not cease flowing. In this way Elijah, and she, and her child had food for many days. The Father in heaven had provided for her. This widow had also been remembered by the Lord. Her despair receded and her faith returned.

And then? Not long after, her little boy became critically ill. He gradually lost strength and finally died. Again the widow of Zarephath despaired. His death now seemed a terrible thing to her, although she had shortly before grimly determined to lay herself and her child upon a cot, there to invite death. And now that it had happened, she grieved. Her conscience troubled her, for she asked Elijah, "Art thou come unto me to call my sin to remembrance, and to slay my son?" She felt that God's overawing majesty had settled upon her home, that her child's death had been God's punishment for her sin. That man of God, she thought, had looked into her heart and had detected that it was sinful. Therefore the vengeance of God had come upon her.

Her soul grew grim and bitter again. She longed to reproach Elijah. But God did not let her persist. He allowed Elijah to perfect another miracle. The prophet came from the stairs with the child in his arms, gave him to his mother, and said, "See, thy son liveth." Then her faith returned with a fervent vigor. She praised God in gratitude, and exclaimed: "By this I know that thou art a man of God, and that the word of the Lord in thy mouth is truth."

Suggested Questions for Study and Discussion

1. How did God first test the faith of this woman?
2. Does this study prove that God careth for His own?
3. Did God again try her faith? Had it been strengthened?

JEZEBEL

But there was none like unto Ahab, which did sell himself to work wickedness in the sight of the Lord, whom Jezebel his wife stirred up.—I KINGS 21:25

READ — I KINGS 21

SIDON and Tyre, in Jesus' estimate, were about the equals of Sodom and Gomorrah. These were two commercial cities, situated on the coast of the Mediterranean Sea, just north of Palestine. Both cities rolled in wealth. This prosperity fomented all kinds of sensual entertainment, and for that reason Tyre and Sidon were reputed to be centers of vice and ungodliness.

Jezebel came from Sidon. She was a princess, the daughter of Ethbaal, King of Sidon. You can imagine what a contrast it was to Jezebel, accustomed as she was to beautiful Sidon, in which waves of licentious delight were constantly welling up, to move to rural Jezreel, with its simple life and its service of Jehovah.

It is true that Jeroboam had instituted the service of the golden calves, but it is also true that that wor-

ship was still intended to serve Jehovah. The Church
had been falsified, we might say, but it was still the
Church of Sinai. For that reason the prevailing tone
of life in Israel was too rigorous and too lean for a
sensation-seeker such as Jezebel was.

She could never have endured Samaria as it was.
But she was not worrying. She would change things!
Ahab, her husband, was a spineless, cowardly man.
She could wrap him around her thumb. It would not
be long, she surmised, before Jezebel would be the
feared commander in Israel.

Her plan was comparatively simple. Samaria was
to be converted into a Sidon. To that end the extravagant and sinful worship of Baal was to be substituted
for the service of Jehovah. In other words, the service of Jehovah was to be suppressed, and therefore,
the prophets had to be murdered. Thus there began
that strenuous conflict between Jehovah and Baal as
it was fought, respectively, between Elijah and Jezebel. For it was Jezebel who constantly instigated her
husband to do evil.

Beautiful temples were erected everywhere in honor
of Baal. Priests walked about in gorgeous trappings
and set the mouths of the masses agape. Extravagant
banquets and gay carousals were introduced. And,
inasmuch as the service of Jehovah had already become contaminated by many alien ingredients, the
people were easily induced to follow where Jezebel led.
The prophets were murdered. Elijah had to flee. He
said that he could not find a single man or a single
woman who still feared God. We know that there were
still seven thousand who did. But these did not know
each other. They had to keep their faith a secret, and

for that reason they did not know each other. That effectively Jezebel had struck fear into their hearts.

How valiantly Elijah fought for Jehovah, and how glorious God's omnipotence proved to be upon Carmel are matters which do not concern us. Jezebel demands all of our attention. She had no conscience and she had no heart. Arrogance and sensuality kill all that is human in people; they silence the voice of conscience, and they petrify the hearts of men. They did so in Sidon and they did so in Jezebel. That is perfectly obvious from the coolly calculating manner in which she went about the killing of the prophets. Because her conscience was silent she put Naboth to death after a trial for which the witnesses had been bribed. Later, when Ahab had been fatally wounded by the arrow, she indifferently posed as a charming and tempting woman. When Jehu entered the city she placed herself before the window, and wantonly tried to entice him into her net (II Kings 9:30).

How gruesomely revolting she was! A woman can become that insidious. God gives her a rich and loving nature. Women who know how to develop these gifts can bless our lives more than ever a man could attempt to do. But once a woman gives up her high calling, she sinks more deeply into bogs of sin than it is possible for a man to sink. Her brutality becomes that of a tigress. Her shamelessness becomes base venality. And if she happens to be a woman who has a strong personality, she becomes a fiendishly wicked murderess such as Jezebel was.

There are more heartless men than heartless women, but a heartless woman is far more dangerous. Even a peerlessly wicked Ahab seems meek when compared with the fanatic blasphemy of this disgraceful woman. Many a martyr for God's cause was compelled to seal his testimony with his life because of her relentlessly searching eye. The poison which that woman injected into the blood of the Ten Tribes coursed in their veins for centuries. Her responsibility will be proved very heavy when she shall be sometime judged before the seat of Christ. She will be cursed for what she did to His prophets.

That eternal judgment will be far severer than that which she received on earth. Yet this, too, was terrible in itself. She was pushed from the window at which she exhibited her wickedness. Her body crashed to the cobblestones. Her corpse was deemed too foul for burial. It was left lying in the congealed blood that oozed from it. The wild dogs crept from the woods, lapped that blood, and tore the rotten flesh from her bones. Of Jezebel there remained only a skull and the skeletons of her hands and feet.

Suggested Questions for Study and Discussion
1. In what environment was Jezebel reared?
2. What plans did she lay and carry out?
3. Did her influence affect the later life of the Israelites?

THE SHUNAMMITE

And it fell on a day that Elisha passed to Shunem, where was a great woman, and she constrained him to eat bread.—II KINGS 4:8

READ — II KINGS 4: 8-37

THE service of the priests and Levites had not been retained in the Ten Tribes. For that reason the God-fearing people of Israel esteemed the prophets highly, and for the same reason the prophets of Israel were more significant men than those of Judah. Judah never learned to know such extraordinarily qualified personalities as those of Elijah and Elisha. It need not surprise us, therefore, that the pious people of Israel dearly loved these men.

The woman of Shunem gives us a typical example of such love. Elisha frequently passed through Shunem on his perodic journeys from Carmel, where he lived, to Jezreel, the capital. At first he regularly made this journey in a single day. But, as he became older, that trip became too fatiguing for him. One of Shunem's prominent women noticed this, and esteemed it an honor and a privilege to extend hospitality to the man of God. After that Elisha regularly stayed at her house as he journeyed through.

She had married a comparatively old man when she herself was still rather young. So striking was the difference between their ages that Elisha explained her childlessness by reference to her husband's age. "She hath no child and her husband is old," he said. Such marriages are uncommon. Yet, it can be quite easily understood that there are women who like to give their love to an older man. In general, there are perhaps two reasons for this. First, there is the indisputable fact that young women mature earlier than young men. Such women do not detect "man enough" in the young men of their age, they find nothing in them which they "can look up to." Men of their own age have not enough of masterliness and solidity to give the women they associate with a feeling of appropriate inferiority. And to this must be added the fact that some women, because of their natures, are inclined to look for "fatherly" characteristics more than for "manly" ones. Women such as these will be more impressed by men of a more advanced age.

The Shunammite was such a woman. On the one hand, she had that readiness which would have enabled her to get along splendidly alone. And, on the other hand, she felt inclined to attach herself to one whom she could look up to as a father. She expressed this last named trait by her marriage to a man older than herself, and by her offer of hospitality to the aged Elisha. Yes, she might have made her own way in the world. But she was a woman, and felt the need of attaching her faith to Elisha.

Her independence and readiness are, however, quite as obvious in her activities. She planned everything and put everything into effect. It was she who induced Elisha to enter her home. She conceived of the plan to build a little prophet's office for him. She cared for the sick child, and when he died, she allowed herself no rest until she had gone to Carmel, induced Elisha to return with her, and asked him to restore her child to life.

It is rather remarkable that a woman who served as a kind of community mother, should combine with her maternal devotion a daughter's tendency to lean upon an old man like Elisha. She knew her appropriate place. She asked her husband's permission for and approval of all she did. And yet, in this family the husband seems to have been rather superfluous. The wife was the active and responsible person in the home.

As a mother she cared for Elisha and arranged

matters in a way which enabled the old prophet to appropriately spend occasional nights at her house. As
a mother she was loved by her community. She could
truly say, "I dwell among mine own people." Hence,
when this capable and energetic woman was asked to
state her most intimate wish, she immediately revealed
that she wanted most of all to become a mother. Her
faith was active when she asked for that child. And
when he died, she leaned so strongly upon that faith,
that she dared to ask God's omnipotence for a miracle.
By restoring her child to her, God confirmed the
sincerity and validity of that marvelous faith.

Suggested Questions for Study and Discussion

1. Why did the prophets receive higher esteem
   among the Ten Tribes?
2. How can you say that this woman was a type of
   community mother?

NAAMAN'S WIFE'S LITTLE JEWISH MAID

*And the Syrians had gone out by companies, and
had brought away captive out of the land of Israel
a little maid; and she waited on Naaman's wife.*
—II KINGS 5:2

READ II KINGS 5

WHAT to us are maidservants, formerly, in heathen
countries, were bondwomen, girls who were born of
slaves, who were taken in war, or were purchased on
the market. But there was also a lower class of servants, who worked in the fields and stables. These
ranked far below the house servants in the social scheme
of that day. Think, for instance, of the high positions

held by Hagar and Zilpah. Today we would call such women ladies-in-waiting. The little Jewish girl which Naaman gave to his wife served in this capacity.

Naaman was the commander-in-chief of the army of the King of Syria. He was that in the sense that he served at once as the minister of war and as the general of the army. He was, therefore, a man of high rank. The glory of his position increased when he succeeded in defeating Israel, and when he returned to Damascus heavily loaded with the spoils of war. Naturally, he could select for himself just what he wanted of those spoils. Accordingly, he had, upon his wife's request, appropriated to himself a ready little Jewish girl, whom he gave his wife as a maid-in-waiting.

This commander-in-chief constantly suffered because of an annoying disease. It was not the genuine leprosy of which Leviticus speaks, but it was, nevertheless, tantalizing and severe. The disease did not hinder him from fulfilling his duty as a general, but it relentlessly annoyed him.

It was natural that the little Jewess should hear of her lord's disease after a while. Therefore, as soon as she had grown somewhat more intimate with her mistress, she told her that there was a prophet in her country who did miracles, and who could certainly cure the general of his illness. Naaman's wife told her husband. He took the hint, asked the king for a safe-conduct, and went to Samaria. There Israel's king directed him to Carmel. He found complete recovery with Elisha. Thanks to this remarkable recovery, Jehovah, the God of Israel, Who alone can do miracles, was praised at Damascus. Israel had no fear of attack by the Syrians as long as Naaman was commander-in-chief.

This fascinating narrative teaches us first of all that the scope of a maid's influence can be far-reaching. It can affect the destinies of peoples and of nations. Even though that influence may not always prove to be as significant as it was in the case of this maidservant, yet every servant has no reason to think that he or she is of no importance. Maidservants exert an influence for better or for worse, sometimes upon their fellow-servants, sometimes upon the children in the home, and sometimes upon their masters and mistresses. If only we could calculate the scope of that influence! We should marvel at the tremendous effects which a servant girl can produce upon her environment. Her virtues and her vices, her habits and her peculiarities all leave an indelible influence upon those she meets. The influence exerted upon children is later expressed in the men and women who occupy responsible positions in state and society. We should be amazed to learn that many of the happenings which occur in the prominent sphere of activity borrow their impetus from the influence some servant girl long ago exerted upon those about her. Servants who appreciate this fact will know that their significance is not as mean as it may sometimes seem to be. A Christian maid, who fears God, will have an appropriate sense of her responsibility. And this holds true not for ladies-in-waiting only, but also especially for nursemaids. The influence exerted upon the impressionable minds of children become conclusively significant for life.

The example of Naaman's little Jewess has, however, a special significance. She served God, and was occupied in a heathen family. She had not entered Naaman's home by choice. God had permitted her to be taken captive in war, had brought her to Damascus, and had introduced her to this prominent family. There she took the risk of speaking to her pagan mistress about her God, the God of Israel. She prudently chose occasion for her comment, by making it only after she could take a sympathetic and sincere interest in a member of the family.

Christian maidservants should take her as their example. It is a disappointing fact that so many of these serve in heathen homes, and that in spite of that, so very few of the members of these homes ever become converted. The older church chronicles are packed with examples of slaves who saved their masters or mistresses for Christ. It ought to occur as frequently today. We hear of it most unfrequently. There seems to be a want of intimacy between maids and their superiors. All confidential contacts are made impossible by a cultivated aloofness. The slaves of an earlier day fostered no such attitude, but tried to cultivate a reciprocal confidence. When we observe the modest and tactful, the ingratiating and lovable manner in which this Jewess fulfilled her responsibility, the question is raised whether much might not be gained for Christ if our maidservants cultivated a humbler attitude toward and a more spontaneous love for the people they serve.

The Jewish girl in the royal palace of General Naaman at Damascus did not snub confidential advances. She fostered them by her sincere and devoted love.

Suggested Questions for Study and Discussion

1. How was it that this girl came into the employ of the wife of Naaman?
2. In what way could this Jewish girl reveal her faith?
3. What was the result of this testimony to the people of Israel?
4. What should this example lead us to do?

ATHALIAH

And when Athaliah the mother of Ahaziah saw that her son was dead, she arose and destroyed all the seed royal.—II KINGS 11:1

READ — II CHRONICLES 22

THERE is a striking parellelism between Israel's relationship to Judah and that of Cain's descendants to those of Seth. Cain separated himself and his family from the God-fearing people of his day. Years later the sensual daughters of the Cainites tempted the sons of Seth and thus prepared for the flood. In this same way idolatrous Israel first segregated itself from Judah. Later, by means of a licentious woman, it tried to snare Judah into its net, and thus prepared it for the Babylonian exile.

The licentious woman who was in this way to cause Judah's moral life to decay was Athaliah, the daughter of Ahab and Jezebel. She personified all the evil of her ill-famed parents. Jezebel had brought poison from Sidon and injected it into the veins of Israel. And now Athaliah was to transfuse some of that same poison into Jerusalem's veins.

Nothing permits us to think that Judah ever exerted

a good influence upon Israel. But we have good reasons
to know that evil influences frequently were exerted
by Israel upon Judah. We notice that in this narrative
that a king of the House of David, so far from choos-
ing to ally himself with God's prophet in the crucial
conflict between Ahab and Elijah, chose instead to intimately ally himself with Ahab's dynasty. He even
permitted Joram, the Crown Prince, to marry Jezebel's
daughter.

Had Jerusalem not already departed widely from
the service of Jehovah, the coming of Athaliah and
her priests of Baal would have incited a violent reaction among the people at Jerusalem. But no such reaction occurred. On the contrary, Athaliah became
the ruler of Israel the moment she was made queen.
Her every gesture was obeyed.

In order to execute her plans she exercised her reckless power at will. The Temple of Jehovah was practically closed. Resplendent Baal-temples sprang up
everywhere, just as they had in Israel at Jezebel's
command. Mattan served as the highpriest of Baal.
Naturally, such innovations changed the tenor of the
life at Jerusalem. Worldliness soon prevailed and the
last remnant of the fear of the Lord seemed to depart
from Jerusalem's walls. So intriguing and persistent
was this infamous woman's designs, that she intentionally sought to inculcate her pernicious motives into her
son. She hoped that he and his generations after him
would continue the process of Baalizing Jerusalem.
Thus she planned that Baal-worship would become
firmly established in Judah. Had she succeeded in her
plans, Jerusalem could not have hoped to escape that
curse.

But the Lord called Jehu. He annihilated Ahab's dynasty in Israel and put Athaliah's son, Ahaziah, to death. That catastrophe did not, however, restrain Athaliah from persisting in her designs. As the situation was, another of Joram's sons, one not trained by her, would succeed to the throne. This was a circumstance which indeed portended evil for Athaliah's schemes. But she made short work of that. She commanded that all of Joram's sons be killed. Had that command been completely fulfilled, David's generations would have terminated. Athaliah knew that as a queen she could marry some pagan prince. Thus she would make the worship of Baal an eternal verity in Israel.

The Lord obstructed her progress. By a miracle the little Joash was rescued from the massacre of the princes. Later, the highpriest, Jehoiada, seized the courage to publicly crown him king. When Athaliah on that occasion profaned the temple, he had the captains seize her, drag her out of the sanctuary, and put her to death. Thus her diabolical schemes failed. David's House was not destroyed. The Messiah was born from Jesse's generations. But that does not make Athaliah a less revolting figure. Her evil passion and despicable arrogance induced her to deliberately poison a people. She was so wicked that when fortune threatened to hinder her progress, she did not hesitate to exterminate all the royal seed.

It is a tragic fact that the scope of a woman's evil influence is broader than that of her good effects. It is true that a woman in a responsible position can exert a wide influence for good. Yet, because of her nature and because of her Divinely appointed function that influence must necessarily remain rather limited. But when a woman fails to be limited by her nature, and when she refuses to be curbed by the limitations God has fixed, her influence, just because of that diabolical pride becomes that much more dangerous.

The good which a single woman achieved has never equaled the evil accomplished by Jezebel and Athaliah. And, as it was in Israel it has remained throughout history. A woman bent on destruction has always proved doubly dangerous. It is so today. A pagan woman who seeks to destroy is far more effective than a Christian woman who tries to save. It is the old story of Paradise. It was Eve who tempted Adam.

Suggested Questions for Study and Discussion

1. What religion did Athaliah propagate?
2. How did she try to blot out all fear of God?
3. Did God stay her hand, and so help His people?

JEHOSHEBA

But Jehosheba, the daughter of King Joram, sister of Ahaziah, took Joash the son of Ahaziah, and stole him from among the king's sons which were slain; and they hid him, even him and his nurse, in the bed-chamber, from Athaliah, so that he was not slain.—II KINGS 11:2

READ II KINGS 11

THE coming of the Mediator in human form has repeatedly been seriously threatened. It was threatened by the fact that the first Patriarch remained childless, by Jacob's flight, by Saul's attempt to pin David to the wall, and again, and not least, by Athaliah's attempted massacre of the royal seed. It cannot be

said, of course, that Athaliah planned that massacre
with the deliberate intention of preventing the coming
of the Mediator. But Satan, doubtless, did have this
purpose in mind when he instigated her to undertake
that act. And when Athaliah commanded that the king's
sons be slain, she served as a tool in Satan's hand.
Imagine for a moment, that Athaliah had succeeded
in her plans, and that all of Ahaziah's sons had
been murdered. Then Jesse's generations would have
terminated, and God's promises would have wanted
fulfillment.

Jehosheba saved Joash's life. By rescuing the life
of that little prince she rescued the hope of Israel, and
thwarted Satan's attempt to prevent the glorious event
of Bethlehem. But, just as we had no reason to believe
that Athaliah consciously tried to interfere with Christ's
coming, so we cannot suppose that Jehosheba's effort
to save Joash was her conscious attempt to make Bethlehem sure. Athaliah was Satan's tool, and Jehosheba
was God's. Athaliah's work was destined to fail, because Satan is impotent against God's purposes, and
Jehosheba had to succeed because God's plans are
invariably realized.

Jehosheba was a princess, the daughter of King
Joram. She had married Jehoiada, the highpriest. In
our day we observe that noble women of high standing frequently marry Ministers of the Word. Service
in that holy work causes all class distinctions to van-
ish. In this same sense, Jehosheba, although she was
a king's daughter and a king's sister, married a de-
scendant of Levi, the head of the priest class in Judah.
As Jehoiada's wife she lived in the Temple, not in the
Palace. The right to search the Temple was outside

the jurisdiction of the state, and for that reason, once she had determined to save the prince's life, she decided to hide him in one of the bedchambers of the Temple.

The Scriptures do not state how she happened to secure Joash. It seems that his nurse assisted her. Perhaps this is the most faithful representation of the circumstances: Jehosheba was the wife of Jehoiada, and we have that reason and others to believe that she feared God. She must have learned that Joash's nurse had also kept the faith; and in those trying times these women had sought each other's company. This, doubtless, gave Jehosheba an occasion to persuade the nurse to flee to the Temple with the baby. Athaliah, at least, did not detect what had happened. She supposed that the whole of David's family had been killed. Hence, when Joash was made king four years later, Athaliah expressed her surprise by shouting "Treason! Treason!"

Jehosheba's name ought, therefore, to be kept in grateful remembrance by the Church of the New Testament. Hers was a most appealing character. She did not crave for mundane luxuries. Even though Ahaziah was her brother, and though the life of splendor at a royal court might have been hers, she chose, in preference to that, a secluded life in the House of God. Her calm and somewhat introspective character had developed in her a courage unequaled by men. It was not Jehoiada the priest who tried to save David's generations from annihilation. For fear's sake he would have permitted the whole royal family to be killed. Of all the men at Jerusalem, who at that time still feared Jehovah's name, not one dared to assert

his position. They would have liked to, but they did
not dare. They lacked the courage. And while all
these men, including the highpriest, feared to act, Jehosheba did the courageous thing. She grasped the
full significance of the situation, and acted courage-
ously and conclusively. It was a dangerous thing to
do. If Athaliah had heard of it, she would most certainly have killed Jehosheba. But she had made up
her mind, was determined, and after that she never
once hesitated.

Her courage and readiness seem to have impressed
her husband so forcibly, that he, six years later, displayed the same brave initiative. He dared to crown
Joash king, and to execute God's judgment upon Athaliah.

Suggested Questions for Study and Discussion

1. How was the coming of the Mediator threatened?
2. How did she save the life of the little prince?
3. Did the faith and courage of this woman tend to
   strengthen that of her husband in crowning the
   king?

H U L D A

*So Hilkiah the priest, and Ahikam, and Achbor,
and Shapran, and Asahiah, went unto Hulda the
prophetess, the wife of Shallum the son of Tikavah,
the son of Harhas, keeper of the wardrobe; (now
she dwelt in Jerusalem in the college); and they
communed with her.*—II KINGS 22:14

READ — II KINGS 22:14-20; II CHRONICLES 34:21-33

Women naturally rise to a position of greater prominence in an age, a generation, or a nation in which

masculine vigor is wanting. As such times they gain a wonderful scope of influence, be it for better or for worse. Not only does their influence involve a larger scope, but it even seems that they are then given added qualities and capacities, and positions of honor and prominence pass from the men to the women. This circumstance held true in the last days which preceded the fall of Rome. It was true in France just before the great Revolution. At present three queens are ruling, and women are gradually becoming prominent in cultural and scientific pursuits. So it was, too, when the state of Israel began to totter. That is obvious from the detrimental influences that proceeded from Jezebel and Athaliah. It is obvious also from Hulda's championship of Jehovah.

Once before in the crisis of national disintegration a Deborah had arisen to inspire a Barak to action. But after that time and throughout Israel's golden age, women had remained in the background. Finally, because masculine initiative was lacking, Jezebel and Athaliah rose to accelerate destruction's pace. And then, again because there was no champion among the men, Jehosheba and Hulda asserted themselves, each in her own way, to thwart the force of that destruction. Jehosheba did so by preserving the sacred lineage, and Hulda by testifying for Jehovah's name.

We know that God usually chooses men to be His representatives in public service. Only a man could serve as a priest in Israel. Even the sacrificial lamb had to be a male. Except for Athaliah, Israel and Judah had no ruling queens. Throughout the centuries prophets, not prophetesses, arose to acquaint Israel with the burden of the Lord. This last circumstance is particularly significant when one compares it with the tendency of Pagan peoples to seek their fortune-tellers among the women. The soothsayers in superstitious circles are generally women. The witches of whom we read were women. In highly cultured Greece the person who spoke for the renowned oracle at Delphi was Pythia, a woman. It seems natural that it should be thus. The qualities of the personality that are expressed in such pursuits are a subjective mood, a sensitive imagination, a lively susceptibility to impressions, and the ability to detach one's personality from one's self. These are the very characteristics which stand opposed to a vigorous, rational discipline and to a concentrated will. Hence, if you were asked whose personality is the better adapted to the work of prophecy, the woman's or the man's, you would immediately reply that that profession seems more peculiarly appropriate to a woman. She is peculiarly subject to rapture and ecstacy. And, indeed, in superstitious circles, the woman is entrusted with the work of prophecy. But in the sphere of faith the situation is exactly reversed. There the instruments of faith have almost exclusively been men. Only Deborah and Hulda are named as prophetesses. The former prophesied in the period of disintegration which followed Joshua's leadership, and the latter in that which ensued upon Ahab's evil reign.

Hulda's efforts seem to have been extraordinarily blessed. Hezekiah had finally reacted against the moral and spiritual dissolution which followed in Athaliah's wake. But that reaction was not yet effectual. Under Manasseh it waned again, and the spiritual morale rapidly deteriorated. At the time of his death reformation was critically necessary.

In Josiah's beautiful reign, it was, doubtless, his mother Jedidah, but to an even larger extent the prophetess Hulda who inspired the king to reform the pagan condition of the state. Hulda was an ordinary peasant woman. She was married to Shallum, of whom we know nothing besides. In spite of her humble background, however, she was so highly reputed that the king sent the highpriest, together with some of his ministers, to ask God's will of her. And the narrative specifically assures us that because of her prophecy Josiah was induced to renew the Covenant with Jehovah.

God repeatedly acts in this way. Villages could be pointed out in our country where it was thought that the cause of the Lord was lost because men lacked the spirit of championship. Then the Lord appointed a simple woman, inspired her not only to become his child, but also to publicly witness for His name. Thereupon the pious people of her community rallied around her, and because of the fervor she displayed, God's church was reinspired for many miles about. These are the Huldas of our day. They arise in a period of ecclesiastical decay. And they inconspicuously disappear again when they have completed their beautiful work.

Suggested Questions for Study and Discussion

1. Why did women and Huldah in particular, rise to prominence at this time?
2. In what way did Hulda serve?
3. In what way is she an example to us?

NOADIAH

My God, think thou upon Tobiah and Sanballat according to these their works, and on the prophetess Noadiah, and the rest of the prophets that would have put me to fear.—NEH. 6:14

READ — NEHEMIAH 6

Noadiah stands beside or, if you choose, over against Hulda. Both are called prophetesses in the Scriptures. But there was this difference between them. Hulda inspired the reformation that was begun by Josiah, and Noadiah obstructed the reformation that was carried on by Nehemiah. Hulda was a true prophetess and Noadiah was a false one. What in Hulda was inspired by the Spirit, in Noadiah was merely the product of the subjective imagination.

God spoke directly to the prophets and prophetesses, we know, but something else besides that Divine inspiration was active in them. They were usually made subject to a spiritual ecstacy. That ecstacy was partly the result of the inspiration of the Spirit, partly the product of their natural temperaments and dispositions, and partly the effect of deliberate cultivation. We know, for instance, that there were schools of the prophets and that music occupied a prominent position in the curriculum of each of these.

This mediate aspect of prophecy served as the reason for many false prophets to arise. There were men and women whose temperaments were by nature easily excited, who were inclined to work themselves into a state of unnatural fervor, and who then went about the country with this self-incited fervor, imitating God's speech. These were people whose general disposition must have resembled some we know, resembled those among us who grow very ardent about a hectic conversion, but in whom all the ardor and enthusiasm is merely the product of their own subjective selves.

Noadiah was not a pious woman who had meditated much upon holy matters. She had simply pursued the direction suggested by her natural temperament. She compensated for a want of the Spirit's dictation by an excess of false excitement. Thus she palmed-off the pseudo-ecstacy of her own feelings for the Word of God.

Such a practice made Noadiah an exceptionally and dangerously effective woman. Such pseudo-pious, nervously excited women generally make an effective impression. They speak with what seems to be a sincere and zealous passion. There is fervor in their eyes. And by their speech the masses are induced to believe that they are gifted with Divine revelation. Hence, when Noadiah assisted Tobiah and Sanballat in hindering Nehemiah's efforts at reformation, you can easily imagine how she went about it. She must have suggested something like the following:

"The situation was simply serious. The Temple lay in ruins. Jerusalem's walls were shattered. Reformation was certainly in order, and in God's own time it ought certainly to be begun. Just now Israel had to remain under the curse of God's punishment. True humility demanded of them that they gladly and willingly bow to the burden God had placed upon them as the result of their sins. And what did that man Nehemiah, propose to do. Why, he wanted to personally institute a reform, and that immediately. Those

were merely human efforts, mere human plans. God
would certainly thwart their progress. Beware Nehemiah, lest the sword overtake you as you proceed
with your proud endeavors."

And to many of the thoughtless people to whom
she spoke her words seemed surcharged with piety.
How neatly she had stated the matter! Yes, indeed!
God's curse threatened Jerusalem. Beware of those
proud, human efforts. Of course, God would begin the
reformation in his own good time. Down with Nehemiah and all his self-designed efforts at reformation.

Do not think for a moment that Nehemiah was
not annoyed by these false prophecies. If a priest of
Baal or a priestess of Melecheth had stood before him,
they would have precipitated more vigorous efforts on
his part. But Noadiah was discouraging the people
by falsely pious chatter, and her language sometimes
caused his own feelings to become discouraged. It
was hard for him to keep up the courage of all the
people, alone. Strenuous conflicts were being fought
in his soul. And always those words echoed in his
ears, "Mere human efforts!" These sapped his spiritual strength.

What did he do? Engage in debate with Noadiah?
Point out her folly and try to undermine her position
by logic and demonstrations? He pursued a better
course against her than that. He prayed against her.
He knew that that was his sole weapon against her.
Therefore he prayed, "My, God, think upon Tobiah and
Sanballat, and on the prophetess Noadiah, who would
have put me in fear."

That prayer was answered. Because of it Noadiah

was disarmed. Nehemiah persevered, and, by God's grace, the work of reformation progressed rapidly. The Reformation of the sixteenth century also met women who possessed a piety and tried to weaken the strength of the heroes of faith. They tried to do it by bandying about the same phrases that Noadiah used, phrases such as "a judgment of God" and "merely human efforts." At every reformation of the church these women are present to hinder progress. And only those men resist it successfully who, like Nehemiah, appreciate that nothing is gained against such enemies by debate, but that much is wrought by prayer against them.

Suggested Questions for Study and Discussion

1. How did Noadiah compare with Hulda as a prophetess?
2. How did Nehemiah overcome Noadiah? Could we not use the same weapon?
3. What can each of us learn from this study?

VASHTI

But the queen Vashti refused to come at the king's commandment by his chamberlains: therefore was the king very wroth and his anger burned within him.—ESTHER 1:12

READ — ESTHER 1

Vashti is one of the nobler women of humanity. True, she refused to obey her king and husband Ahasuerus, but who dares to say that there are not instances in which a wife, especially a wife in a prominent position, may not sometimes disobey? An im-

pressive festivity was being held in the capitol of the
Persian empire. Its splendor was such that it still
seeks an equal. Thousands of people participated in
the banquet. It was prolonged for seven days in order that all who came from every part of the empire might be accommodated at the tables. At most
of the tables, therefore, one guest rose to make room
for another. But at the central table the group remained constant. There the king and his dignitaries
indulged a whole week of constant festivity. It may
be that men in that day were stronger than they are
now, but the inference is safely made, that they, too,
after seven days of successive banqueting and carou-
sal, had reached a state of semi-intoxication. At least,
we may believe that that is the import of the biblical
phrase, "the heart of the king was merry with wine."

In that intoxicated condition the king commanded
that the queen be brought. He wanted to exhibit her
beauty to the assembled dignitaries. He wanted those
jubilant lords to "feast their eyes on her." That she
was beautiful and that the king summoned her in
order to display that beauty is obvious from the biblical statement to the effect that he called her in order
"to show her beauty."

No woman who possessed a particle of feminine
pride could have obeyed that summons. Not even a
European queen could have assented to that, although
in Europe the queens are expected to sit at the tables
with the lords. But, in Persia, social forms dictated
that the queen remain secluded. She never appeared
publicly at banquets. Therefore the request was even
more revolting to Vashti's sense of propriety than it
would have been to some queen in Europe. It is true

that the king had perhaps made the request in a whimsical and capricious moment. Talk had flowed freely at the table, in a drunken moment Ahasuerus had bragged about the beauty of his wife, and he thereupon felt obliged to make good his claims by a demonstration. Accordingly, he had sent for her. If Vashti had been a vain and wanton woman she would, perhaps, have welcomed this opportunity. To such a woman being marveled at constitutes the one worthwhile thing in life. But Vashti was neither vain, nor wanton. She felt that Ahasuerus was demanding that she surrender her honor. She knew very well what consequences her refusal would entail. In spite of that, however, she refused positively. Thus she proved that she thought more highly of her feminine dignity than of the glamor of her social position.

The Persian king immediately determined to reject her. That is not surprising. The law of God which determined that the wife should be subject to her husband of a law of creation, and as such it has as a tradition of Paradise been observed among all peoples. But, because of sin, God's ordinance to that effect has been robbed of its sacred significance. Men have conceitedly interpreted it as giving them license for tyranny. They have used this law as a weapon by means of which they have enslaved womanhood in almost all non-Christian countries. It is no wonder, then, that all the ministers and officials at that Persian court immediately approved of Vashti's deposition. They felt that if they did not their own wives might appropriate to themselves the independent whims of Vashti.

In Israel alone this ordinance was restored to its

original sacred significance. There women secured a dignified position. Christianity has liberated woman from every bond which might infringe upon her appropriate dignity. Every Christian wife knows that she need not and may not obey her husband in what opposes God's laws, and in what infringes upon her feminine pride. It is true, of course, that there are women who have, in turn, distorted this liberty. In our generation many have rejected this ordinance altogether and have attempted to subjugate man to their tyranny. God will punish them for that, not because it robs man of domains, but because it violates a law He has determined for the relationship of the wife to the husband.

Suggested Questions for Study and Discussion

1. What can we admire in Vashti?
2. Were her actions in accordance with the teachings of the Bible?
3. Were her actions approved according to the standards of Persia?
4. What does this study teach us, and our women in particular?

ESTHER

And he brought up Hadassah, that is Esther, his uncle's daughter: for she had neither father nor mother, and the maid was fair and beautiful; whom Mordecai, when her father and mother were dead, took for his own daughter.—ESTHER 2:7

READ — ESTHER 2

Esther, the last woman of the Old Testament of whom we intimately know anything, does not impress us favorably. In fact, she serves to illustrate how far Israel had degenerated while in exile.

We have abundant reasons to know that she was very beautiful. After Ahasuerus had combed the country from India to the Mediterranean Sea for the most beautiful maidens, she was regarded by him as the most beautiful. She most completely captivated the Persian ruler and was made the queen in Vashti's stead.

Besides her beauty, there are two other qualities of her character which please us. The first of these is her tender affection for Mordecai, her foster-father, and the second is the decisive courage with which she opposed Haman. There are many who, when they are suddenly raised from obscurity to prominence, become just proud enough to completely ignore their families and those who formerly helped them. Esther displayed a sturdier nobility than those who do that. She had the courage to honor and respect the ties of blood and affection, even though these, perhaps tended to detract from her prestige and from the glory of her position.

And Esther makes an equally favorable impression because of the courage and decision with which she opposed the wicked Haman. She risked much by appearing before the king unsummoned. That is obvious from her own statement "If I perish, I perish." And the actions which followed upon that statement were decisively and tactfully taken. She gave expression to an unusually strong personality.

And yet, we should hesitate to add a sincere love for her people to this list of her outstanding qualities. It is true that in one sense that love seems to have been rather pronounced. But we must not forget that she long hesitated before she did anything definite to save her people. Mordecai first had to tell her "Do not think for a moment that your life is not at stake; as a Jewess you, too, will be killed." That first induced her to take action. "Think not with thyself that thou shalt escape in the king's house more than all the Jews" (4:13). Those words deeply affected her, just as did the other message which Mordecai communicated to her "Who knoweth whether thou art. come to the kingdom for such a time as this?"

We cannot avoid concluding that a woman who refrained from saving a whole nation until her own person was threatened, was not particularly willing to sacrifice her life for her people. But there are other disagreeable aspects to her character. These cast a still darker shadow upon her figure. She should not have married Ahasuerus. Vashti had not been deposed for valid reasons. For that reason Esther cannot be praised for assenting to take her place. It cannot be said that it was a beautiful thing in her to become the queen of a heathen prince. For a daughter of Abraham to marry an Oriental king was simply a violation of the seventh commandment. It cannot be objected to this, that she was irresponsible in this matter because the king could do as he chose with whomever he chose to do it. If Esther had wanted to, she could have made a less favorable impression upon him. Thus she could have avoided that marriage. As a matter of fact she demonstrated that it appealed to her.

There was nothing objectionable in her opposition to Haman. That wicked man had completely earned the fate that accrued to him. But five hundred men, including the ten sons of Haman, had already been destroyed in Shushan. Thereupon the king asked Esther whether she desired anything more. Then Esther had the illegitimate boldness to ask that Haman's sons be suspended from the gallows, and that the Jews be given another day in which to wreak vengeance upon their adversaries. As a result a second slaughter occurred, and the Jews slew three hundred additional men in Shushan.

One dislikes to see an expression of such vengeance, especially in a woman. It seems to suggest that Esther embodied some of the bloodthirstiness which later flagrantly cursed the mother of Herod. Hence, there is an immeasurable difference between the Esther of the Old Testament and the Mary of the New. It almost seems as though Esther was to illustrate how Israel would have degenerated if Mary's Child had not been born. God used Mary, but He also used Esther to fulfill his determinate counsel for the redemption of His people. All will be able to understand that, who kneel at Golgotha to praise God for His salvation, although they know that Judas and Caiaphas and Pilate sinned terribly because of that cross.

Suggested Questions for Study and Discussion

1. What are some of the good qualities of Esther?
2. Why, with all her good qualities, does not Esther impress us favorably?
3. Was it wise for Esther to favorably impress the king?

INDEX OF CHARACTERS

TEXTUAL INDEX